LANDSCAPING [illegible] FOR BEGINNERS:

The Ultimate Guide to have a Beautiful, Evergreen and Edible Garden by Planning, Building, and Planting The Outdoor Spaces You have Always dreamed about.

TAMMY SOLOMON & CLOE WYLIE

Table Of Contents

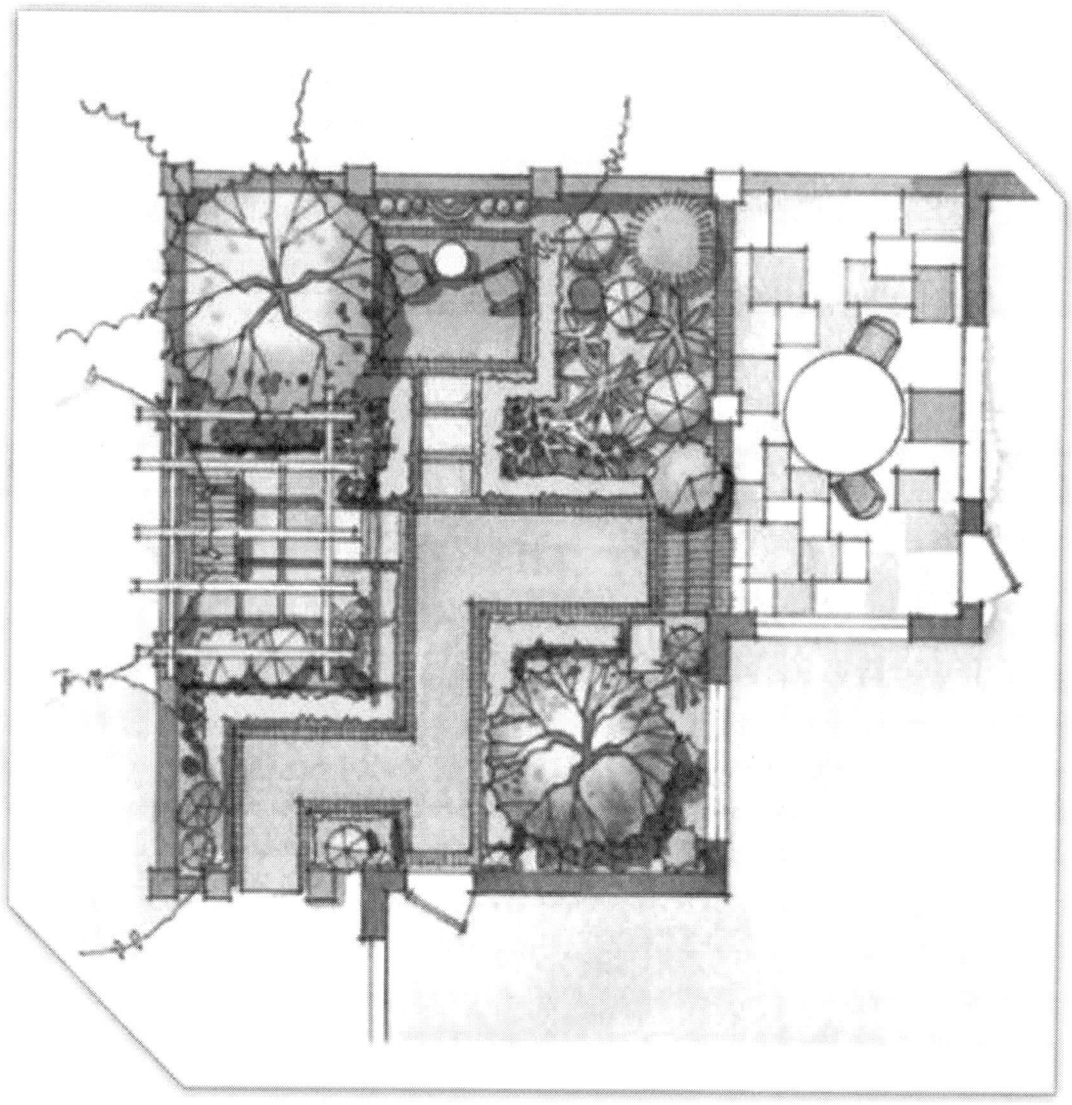

Introduction

Have you ever been sitting — only sitting — in your backyard, wondering, wandering about, and soaking in the view? Never aiming directly at something, just talking of everything and anything to do with your backyard, telling yourself, "What if I placed a tree there?" And, "what will I bring in their place if I transfer those bricks?" It is, in a sense, irrelevant whether you were conscious of this or not because what you have done is to visually make this patch of property your own and come up with concepts and opinions to enhance your outer space.

A lot of people have dreams of having the most amazing front or back yard, the entertaining space to dazzle their friends and be the life of the town and the place to be for social get-togethers but have absolutely no idea of where to begin.

The best place to start is to draw a map, a map, which will be more of a timeline. Take a good long look at where your yard/entertaining space is now and put it at the beginning. Look at catalogs, the internet, local home improvement stores, etc. and find the elements you would like to have and add those. Make sure you're doing this on paper, whiteboard, etc. so you can SEE the path. Believe it or not, this will help you make the best decisions and come to the ultimate conclusion.

Like any other major purchase, you need to have a game plan. You certainly wouldn't buy a house or a car sight-unseen, would you? I didn't think so. Therefore, you need to develop your timeline to make things smooth. Take pictures of elements you like, things you see while you're out and about, or save pictures you see online. Don't make impulse buys or fall for some "Snake oil salesman" when it comes to improving your home. Your home is your castle; treat it as such.

Garden design is the art and method of designing and building plans for gardens and landscapes to be laid out and planted. Garden design can be done by the owners of the garden, or by professionals of varying levels of expertise and experience. Some experienced landscape designers have certain horticultural experience and design standards. Updating the landscaping of your house is a perfect way to improve the worth of your properties and build areas outside for recreation and entertainment. If you choose to concentrate on a reimagined front yard on improving the curb appeal, build a backyard escape on dining and entertaining areas, or both, there are several choices and amenities to consider.

If you also belong to the category of people who aspire to have a well-manicured garden, then don't look elsewhere because you are reading the right book. In this book, we shall deal in detail with that essential aspect of gardening – namely landscaping. Every form of art needs planning, and every garden needs landscaping. Everyone can take up landscaping as a hobby! This book will help you with that, and it will help you to take pleasure in watching your garden take shape.

I hope that by the end of this book, you will be inspired enough to have that picture-perfect garden to share with family and friends.

CHAPTER 1:

What Is Landscaping?

Landscaping as art includes expertise in sound design. This ability is the crucial land development highlight since architecture is the essence of landscaping. The landscaper must be aware of the area's correct design and how it can be implemented. Planning is also important because a well-planned landscape allows a productive development of land. Designing is not an easy task for land developers, as it takes into account several aspects of both the area's "hardscape" and "softscape." The hardscape is the designs in the field, the landforms, the shape of the landscape, and the height of the land, while the softscape includes the lawns, shrubs, trees, etc.

The above are only a handful of what landscaping is about. The construction of an area is not easy and needs a great deal of thought. Yet there are people with the ability who are inborn, and others acquire experience in this field too. If you are not one of these people and your yard needs are growing, you should employ the assistance of experts who provide these services

Landscaping is a discipline-oriented to the task of planning, implementing, and preserving the surrounding land of a house. This covers aspects of furniture, landscape, and architectural design but is not restricted to. A successful landscaper demonstrates ingenuity in his work by transforming a natural area into an exclusive, usable setting that suits the homeowners' tastes. It necessitates a basic understanding of intricate designs and botany in that particular location, under weather and terrain limitations and reimbursements.

Landscaping may be a daunting attempt to dive into it for purposes of economical and dedication. However, if you find yourself on this list, the first phase to the landscaping project has already been completed: performing your homework, which is the research, and this book will help you to do so.

You require particular abilities to do landscaping for a profit. It depends on how far you are planning to expand your business. Some landscaping experts only do side tasks related to sustaining the looks of backyards, while others can generate something special and unique. Through using stone blocks, fountains as well as other objects that create a very distinctive look, they will be capable of transforming the landscape from front or back location. If you choose to start your own company or just get landscaping work, these are the qualities you will need to perform well in this industry.

The Importance of Landscaping

Landscapes and enhancements are essential because they contribute meaningfully to our health and quality of life. They provide the greater picture we are living our lives in. Our perception of wellness is enhanced by living within visually appealing and culturally meaningful landforms. Visiting largely unexplored scenery allows people to stay connected with the natural environment and recharge their brains and bodies.

Landscapes play a significant role in the economy is actively funding the tourism and movie industries and improving the 'green and clean' image of any country by providing value to the export markets. High-quality ecosystems can boost local communities by drawing locals and developing in an environment and visitors alike. Agricultural ecosystems promote a variety of critical practices such as cultivation, woodland, and botany.

From lighting systems to rose bushes, top-notch lawn maintenance, and water systems, you will take advantage of better landscaping. Here are primary reasons why landscaping matters:

Prevents Your Land from Deterioration

Erosion is a hazard to every yard. The soil can deviate significantly from the plant species and flower gardens as rain and wind transition along with all your assets. Stones can become demolished in steep places, presenting a risk to the safety of your children. A good landscaping design plan would work with shour structures to help stop deterioration, especially in steep areas. These building materials could be both alluring and operational, helping to keep the soil where it originally belonged, while also supplying the plants and carvings with a lovely structure.

Break Larger Areas into Nooks

When you have a vast estate, creating private places where your neighbors likely will not see in can be hard. Landscape architecture enables even a full yard to separate into isolated and welcoming areas.

The proper design can create an outdoor living space constructed by shrubs and trees to prevent the town's noise and build a sense of being out in natural surroundings. The layout will consider how you manage to use the storage and make the best setting and theme for your needs. Your creativity only limits the options.

Prevents Your Yard from Flooding

Without a stable landscaping strategy, whenever the storm comes in the spring and fall, your lawn could turn into a mud puddle. If you are yard downpours, the seedlings and original land development in your yard can be damaged, while making the area inaccessible. The correct design will prompt rainwater and runoff into an assigned drainage basin while redirecting the water from your plant species.

Adds Worth

Appropriate landscaping creates a cost to a residence. Landscape and bright lights can be the difference between selling your home and not attempting to sell it. Skilled landscaping is anticipated to raise the price of your asset from 10 to 12 percent. If you are considering giving away your home, an inadequately landscaped yard can drastically decrease your property's value.

Curb Call

A well-paved yard makes the residence look as composed like a man in a custom-made suit. However, this is not just about the potted plants: it is also about the shrubbery, trees, and accents. Also, do not downplay your lawn situation. If you give the plant beds and accents all your interest but disregard the lawn, it is still not going to make a difference. The cleaner and more abundant the yard looks, the happier you can act, and the neighbors. You could even encourage your peers to landscape their yards too.

Resource Efficient

You may not recognize that, but professional landscaping can help with your home's energy-efficiency. Skilled landscaping should prepare for shade trees, help your residence stay fresher, and prevent you from operating your air conditioning unit as hard as possible. Windbreaks can be provided by a properly landscaped yard, which significantly reduces the heating costs. Landscaping can also assist in stormwater control, enabling adequate runoff after heavy rainfall or snow melts to avoid flooding.

Serenity

A beautifully landscaped yard would offer you a beautiful, attractive spot to settle down and rest or invite the company to enjoy. That is why it is worth bringing the work into your yard, alone. There are many explanations for the value of landscaping; these are only a handful. A specialist should have expertise in fields such as; when flowers bloom and how large they get, what healthy soil is, how to make your lawn grow green and lush, where to put a walkway that does not harm the flow of stormwater, and how to grade your flowerbeds and yard to prevent floods.

Creates Natural Habitats

Landscape plans should not always be increased maintenance. Many methods use native plants and vegetation to make a stunning ecosystem that thrives season after season. If a design incorporates plants that are local to the tropical, the landscaping would be well suited to accommodate the regular weather shifts without you or the landscaping team needing particular time and consideration.

Treat Your Landscape as a Separate Ecosystem

By the start of a great and intense day, the backyard is more than just a spot to disengage; it is an environmentalist-system in and of itself. The Land's shifting slope shaded zones, and sunshine places have specific requirements to be determined before they can be utilized. Good landscape design considers these considerations and views the yard like an ecosystem, putting the best plants in the right location. The outcome is a layout that plans sewage, erosion, and plant-life sustainability.

Reduces Environmental Impact

You can attach plants and flowers that are not well adapted to the New York conditions while you are growing a flowerbed yourself. You can need to apply nitrogen to the soil to mitigate the impact of the environmental patterns, soil composition, and humidity. Most commonly produced fertilizers are made of environmentally damaging chemicals; although they help, your tropical flowers thrive in the summer months.

Regulatory privileges of Landscapes

Natural Coolants - Grass is much colder than pavement or concrete. This serves as an environmentally safe "climate conditioner." Typically, lawns will be 31 degrees fresher than pavement and 20 degrees fresher than bare earth. Yet wait, there is more to it. Homes shielding by trees will lower overhead temperatures by something like 40 degrees.

Natural cleaners of the environment - Grass perform a crucial function of trapping pollen, particulate matter from smoking, and other contaminants and generate oxygen.

Water Protectors - Safe lawns will trap polluted pollution that may potentially flow into water bodies.

Air purifiers – Grasses consume and decompose co2 into oxygen and fuel. A 50'x50 "lawn produces sufficient oxygen for a family of three.

Disturbance Minimizers – shrubs and plants significantly reduce noise pollution; over hard floors such as asphalt and pavement, they can reduce the emissions by 20 to 30 percent. Turfgrass rates down and removes discharges into water sources. Lawns and ecosystems must remain a niche component of healthy cities, even in areas that have water shortages and are experiencing drought. There is a range of sustainability solutions that will enable the reduction of water use by controlled lawns and ecosystems but still provide significant environmental benefits.

Privileges of Urban Landscapes

A growing body of work is revealing how necessary it is to integrate tree canopies and gardens into towns and cities. They deliver a wide variety of lifestyle advantages that enhance the residents' standard of living.

Psychological and Physical Gains

Equally well understood and recorded are the effects of human contact with plants, trees, and grass. Evidence also has shown that when people communicate with nature or simply experience it from a lens, they feel emotional reduction and healing. Since going outside, adolescents with ADHD tend to be concentrating more (Harvard Health Publications). Employees are often more efficient while dealing with plants in settings, which enhances executive performance.

CHAPTER 2:

How do you begin the process of creating a beautiful landscape garden?

As with any project, it is often the temptation to jump right in and get started without any real idea of what you are going to do when you get there. Of course, you can do that with landscaping as well, but it isn't going to get you very far if you do.

First things first.

The very first thing that you want to do when you are landscaping your yard is to set a goal. Don't just go out there with a bunch of equipment and some rocks then rip up your yard. It won't end well…

That is going to produce the exact opposite effect of what you want it to do. If you know anything at all about accomplishing projects, you know that you need to have a goal to work towards.

What did you have in mind?

Ask yourself what you want your yard to look like, don't just go out there and hope that it develops as you go along because, chances are, it won't develop into anything like you wanted it to.

Is there a place that you want to shade?

Is there a place that you want to be the focal point for the whole yard?

Are there areas that you want to encourage activity, and on the flip side, are there areas where you want to discourage activity?

Do you want any water areas, ponds, waterfall, future hot tub?

Is there anything that you want that you need a professional company to install for you?

These are all the things that you have to keep in mind when you are starting the project. Know what it is you are after, and then go for that.

Count the cost

Once you have a rough idea of what you are going for in your project, sit down and make a list of the things that you will need, and how much it is going to cost to acquire these things.

Are there tools that you will need? Is there a cheaper alternative to a certain kind of rock or plant that you are looking to get?

There is nothing worse than getting a great start on a project, then running out of the funds that you need to complete the project. It ends up staying unfinished, or it will age differently and require more maintenance to keep it all up to date. These are things that you will want to avoid at all cost, and the simple step of calculating the cost will save you major headaches down the road.

Write down everything in the early stages. These can be changed or modified later if need be, but if you have an idea, write it down. This will help you better visualize what it is you are working with when you are actually at the store trying to decide what it is that you need to purchase.

Picture Perfect

The last thing that you are going to want to do on the very outset of your landscaping project is to take some pictures of your yard and the area that you are going to be landscaping.

This is a further reminder and visual that will help you to keep on the right track when you are actually at the store. It will take all the guesswork out of what color you should go with, and how far apart certain things are.

It will also help you provide an actual visual to an employee if you need help choosing something or asking for some advice. You don't need to spend a lot of time standing in the store trying to correctly describe the color of the fence or the other lawn decorations, you can just show them what you are dealing with, and they will be a lot better able to assist you.

PRO TIP: Either find a friend that is a landscaper, or get a professional estimate and show them your plans for your yard, get their input!! These people are professionals that do this for a living, so they will most likely be able to give you advice and opinions on what to do with your yard and yard plans!

Watch that Forecast

Now that you have everything that you need in stock, watch the weather before you get out there and get things in the ground. You can work around some things easily, but others that need time to set or dry, you will want to have plenty of sunshine for those (or at least no rain, dry weather is best for most outdoor landscaping), so make sure you are ready.

If you get hit by light rain, you can keep working, but if you think it might rain, grab a patio tent. Usually used on patios for shade and a nice place to relax, they are built to keep the rain out, so if you need to work just throw one up in your yard over the work area!

Don't tempt fate, when you have a nice day ahead of you, take full advantage of it, and go out there and get your landscaping going. There isn't any reason to put it off, and the sooner you get it underway, the sooner you will have a beautiful yard around you.

Once you start, do not keep persistent with work, because as soon as you slack of you will never end up getting any job done!

Tying It All Together

As with any project that you decide to take on, there are some common mistakes that you need to watch out for, especially as a beginner. In the excitement of making your yard your own, and adding in all of the elements that you want to make it your own, there are still a few things that you need to keep in mind to keep your yard beautiful to the beholder.

A few of the key elements in this art is to watch for the color scheme, repetition, and scaling. We will now take a look at each of these elements, and figure out why they are so important, as well as why you should take the time to adjust them when you are putting your yard together.

Scale

This one may seem to be unimportant at first, but it is one of those things that may seem like a small detail when you are standing in your yard but is a pretty big detail when you are across the street.

Purpose of landscaping is to make the yard look appealing to those around the area, as well as to yourself. There are some things that you will want to watch for, and scaling is one of those things.

You can easily create the illusion that your house is tiny, or that different parts of your yard are out of proportion with other parts of your yard if you are not mindful of where you place what.

Larger pieces should be placed towards the outside of the yard, and smaller fragments around paths and walkways. A singular, large focal point can be placed anywhere in the yard, but it is always better to keep it a careful distance from the house.

Feel free to take a walk across the street and see what it looks like from out there. Take your time and adjust it to get it to be precisely what you want it to be. It is again one of those tedious things that don't seem like a lot of fun on the outset, but it does pay off when you are finally done and looking into your yard from up the street.

Color Scheme.

Something that may not seem that important at the beginning of the project, but one of the most significant factors in giving your yard that finished look, is its color scheme. It will appear to be a lot more put together and finished if you are careful to add in color scheme in various areas.

Ask the employees at the garden center what colors look good together, and how you can tie it into the color of your house. They are trained to know this sort of thing, and they will be happy to assist you; however, you need them to.

This is also a good time to bring in those photographs that you took in preparation. It will be a lot easier to see colors side by side if you are looking at the color right next to what you intend to purchase, instead of guessing the shade that you need to get.

Cleaning up

The first thing that needs to be done before you even decide a theme for your garden is to clean up space. Seldom do we have a realistic idea of how spacious our backyard or lawn is until we clean them up. Begin mowing your lawn to get rid of all the unkempt grass and weeds. Rake it up nicely to remove all the debris. Remember that it is important that you rake your lawn up at the end of fall and winter to get rid of the fallen leaves and snow whether you decide to venture into the landscaping or not.

When it comes to your backyard, remove all the things that you have been dumping for eons and mow your backyard too. Once you are done cleaning up, you will have an exact picture of how much space you have to work with, and you can plan your garden accordingly. Should you skip this step, rest assured that you will be in for a rude shock when you realize that there are space constraints that you may not have anticipated.

Shape and Design

Takes part at the initial planning stage using sketching. It's putting the idea of how you want your lawn to look like as well as how it will relate to the other parts of the garden. Choose whether you need the garden to look formal or casual, whether you need play areas for kids or dining spaces and consider the connections between different parts of the garden with paths and steppingstones to care for the grass. This is the part where you need to be creative and with the great power of imagination to come up with a beautiful design as you want. Lawns can be of different shapes as possible, and so you do not need to be confined to a rectangular or square lawn with narrow flower beds surrounding. Just when you are satisfied with the design on paper, then you can start to make space physically.

Select the Visual of your Garden

Check your view board to find out what new look you want. You may have chosen a lot of one color, or you may have chosen a different theme. It should help you refine what you're searching for by taking these popular features out and seeing what does not suit that. Yet maybe such variations don't matter – perhaps you choose to keep them in, or you've got a relatively large garden that fits other looks.

We see it as helping to think of the garden as either formal (geometric and ordered with straight lines) or casual (free and easy without regularity in planting). Interestingly, since the brain does not have to work hard to interpret the image, the clean lines of the asymmetrical, formal garden may be restful on the eye. Nevertheless, conventional designs tend to enhance boundaries but consider asymmetric style if you want the garden to look wider.

Creation of a Landscape Layout

Choose a piece of paper and draw a diagram of your garden (we find the graph paper is useful when planning to size)—using a measuring tape to precisely quantify all of your garden's critical dimensions and components, including any features or dots defined. Don't forget to identify the position of any pipes or cables — you're going to try to stop them while landscaping, but you're going to have to recognize where they are going to be and make them available. You'll also want to pick up a tracker to monitor your yard's rise and decline, too. Including everything you need to remember and wisely bid your time will hopefully help you from making any expensive errors later on.

Test the Rule and Talk with Neighbors

Planning laws vary from region to region, but typically very strict limits are imposed on what can be achieved in protected areas with the buildings or property listed, and that involves their gardens. The new building is still prone to these limitations, so it is therefore worth checking with the local authority's planning department to ensure that what you want to build is acceptable. And even though you're not doing some major study, it's worth sitting down with your peers and learning it, and all the implications they can face. Chatting with them regarding the possible knock-on consequences of some instances will probably avoid more questions or issues down the line.

Locating Resources

There are several ways to locate the resources you need to have the space of your dreams. You have Google, phone book, referrals, and several websites that will contractors contact you after you fill out the form stating what you're looking for. Don't go with the first one that contacts you. Get at least 3 estimates for whatever the project is and weigh the options. Using the home and car example from above, you wouldn't buy a car from the first lot you go to, would you? I didn't think so.

Any home addition must be considered a major purchase as it affects your home's value. Think of the proverbial "Pebble in the Pond" effect. Before-tax assessment season, you decide to add a fire pit and benches in the back yard. The tax assessor notices this, and your property taxes go up to $300/year. It doesn't sound like much, but unless you're rolling in cash, it can be a major hit.

Now that you have compiled a list of contractors take a couple of days and research each one. Look at both positive and negative reviews. Look them up on BBB.org and see what kind of rating they have if they have any unresolved complaints. If everything checks out, compare them all, and choose the best one. Remember, "You get what you pay for". I have to explain this a lot to potential customers when I go out to do estimates. I tell them all, "Yes, you can go with the cheaper option, and when that fails in 3-5 years, I'll be here."

Once you have the contractors, contact them. Explain your plans and have them come out to give you an estimate. This will provide you with a solid projection of how much it's going to take to get your project done. Then you are one step closer to realizing your dream space.

CHAPTER 3:

How much is garden landscaping?

Budgeting

Setting your budget is one of the most important steps. However, you decide to pay for this new venture; whether it be with credit cards, cash, or financing, you need to have a reasonable budget set aside for it.

Figure out how much you want to add, where you want to add it and go from there. If you know you can only afford to add a retaining wall, for now, then budget as such. If you prefer to have the patio first, then plan accordingly. Never get in over your head.

When deciding on a budget, there are many factors but, again, you have to prioritize. Consider everything you want to have done, write it down and go over the list. What do you have to have done first? What can wait until you save up some more? See where this is going? Put your list on paper, see it, visualize it, and go from there. It gives you a more tangible element to look at. When you can see your goals on paper, your thought process becomes a lot clearer than just going over it in your head.

It is not unusual for people not to have all the financial affairs in place to construct the entire garden in one go. Many landscape contractors are very able to do the building in stages. When you are heading down that path, it's best to get as much rough landscaping completed as you can in one go, and you can use the hiring expense of the machinery and get on with the very sloppy process.

A decent contractor would not rob you out of your budget by not performing the correct amount of job. They 're trying to want to achieve as best as they can, since they realize if they're not doing good with step one, then you won't even call them in to do the rest. There are, of course, unscrupulous companies out there, but pick carefully and do have references and have a peek at their past ventures.

How to work with your contractor?

Until you call them to have a clear understanding of what you want, get a map of scale illustrating what you want, if necessary, and they can be specific the price from it.

Realize the gap between landscape designers and the facilities they sell. Be realistic about how much a garden can cost.

No good entrepreneur minds digging a plant out or moving a pot and something for you. So, if the landscaper provides a set price, they will cost to create the garden within a certain amount of time.

Piling on extra jobs and asking them to do this for free isn't reasonable to them, mainly if they do require additional supplies. Most contractors need stage fees as they order the supplies ahead of time to create your garden and sometimes wind up charging for them until your garden is complete. It is also important that their invoices are charged on time, and they can control their cash flow and fund their expenses and employees.

Low Cost, Low Maintenance Landscaping

Low budget (and sustainable) landscaping is influenced by many factors including climate, the size of the garden, soil condition and regulatory restrictions.

These days, many of us are on a fixed budget and don't have the money or the time for expansive landscaping with large amounts of resources. But with effort and due diligence, we can get the most out of our small, postage-stamp-sized landscapes.

The same long-term planning and gardening principles of great sustainable landscapes can also be applied to your smaller home gardens.

For low cost and low maintenance landscaping, you have to know which plants to plant in a which location. Knowing which plants to plant in which sites will save you money through lower water and fertilizer usage.

Low-maintenance landscaping requires fewer resources and cost much less to take care of. This landscaping will ultimately support beneficial insects and birds and provide you with long-term benefits, including reducing health risks, saving on resources and intense day-to-day care.

While your budget will affect the type of patio you have and the materials you can use, there are ways you can get the look you want more affordably. At the design stage, it's vital NOT to think about your budget. If you worry too much while designing, it will prevent you from coming up with anything good.

CHAPTER 4:

Elements to consider when first planning

Elements of Landscape Design

An important aspect of landscaping, after choosing the right kind of plants, is how you physically design your garden. It is not important if you choose the optimum collection of plants. The beauty of landscaping lies in how you incorporate the different elements. In this chapter, we present you the four important aspects of design that need to be borne in mind while you design your garden.

It is necessary to remove elements that do not include enhancement or effect on architecture. To maintain the environment tidy, orderly and uncluttered, consider what is essential and what is not so. A basic, excellently defined template is one that will make the software easy to manage and develop.

Options

Selections in color, scale, and style will be varied for generating visual appeal. Should not sacrifice convenience, though, solely to build varied variations.

Balance

Anything that is put in a design must bring with it a specific visual weight. Balance is the idea of meaning that sometimes the entire program has weight. A strategy of formal equilibrium would see all sides mimicking each other, whereas informal equilibrium corresponds to similar but not identical. Both can function well.

Importance

Emphasizing areas of the design utilizing form, shape, or color will create attention and guide the eye via the design, but too much focus may seem messy. Areas of organisms are better left alone. Accent places are intended to stand out even within a broader architectural sense. Core plants may help to relax or de-emphasize design forms.

Order

The sequence refers to how shifts are applied in the aspects of plant size, shape as well as texture. Gradual modifications of one component at a time give a smooth, enticing series—abrupt shifts from a tall plant to a small, or a good-textured plant to a rugged one.

Scale / Size

The size of the elements in a landscape is proportion and is relative to how they respond to each other. It will all match the scale of the landscape and the things in it. A fence or tree that is far bigger than the majority of the landscape can draw the attention away from all else.

Harmony

Harmony is the idea that it all fits well. Interconnection is creating cohesion by utilizing links to dynamically link places such as roads, sidewalks, steps, and fences.

Repetition happens as a concept feature unifies, as it exists in many environments. Repeat may be beneficial, so be cautious not to overburden it. Dominance occurs where one common focal point, like a big tree, tends to unify certain places of support.

Proximity

In design, proximity is nothing but the arranging of the different elements to form a group. For instance, to create a hodgepodge effect, you can group two of different kinds of plants. This grouping of plants is usually done to create a visual and colorful statement.

Repetition

You can use repetition in your garden to emphasize the visual statement you wish to make. You could achieve this by planting a single kind of plant in different places within the garden. An exciting way would be to repeat the texture or color or shapes instead of just having a single plant. This creates a bold and interesting visual statement.

Continuation

Continuation is the process by which you create an edge or line that helps in carrying the viewer's eye across the entire space. The line or edge can either be real or implied. You can create these edges along your garden beds to create that impact. You could go ahead and create a small pathway amidst your beds to add to the visual impact you wish to create.

Continuity

Continuity refers to how the different visual elements of your garden complement each other. In other words, it refers to the visual relationships shared by the various plants in your garden. The simplest way to achieve this is to repeat the same design everywhere. This would, however, add a monotonous flavor to your garden. You can achieve continuity by choosing different kinds of plants that complement each other. For instance, you can select plants which belong to the same range of color but have different textures and shapes.

Hedges

Hedges are one way of creating borders either between neighbors or to mark out the total limits of your property. One way that one can play with hedges is to use it to separate different elements of your garden. For example, flower beds can be set apart from the vegetable garden with a hedge.

Fences

Fences can serve both practical and decorative purposes. It can be made out of wood, plastic, metal, or any other reused or repurposed material that you might find attractive. Wrought iron fences lend an elegant and sophisticated feel to space. Wooden fences have a certain old country, rustic appeal. Painted fences can be in block colors or finely worked on as canvasses for brilliant works of art. A plain white fence can serve as a backdrop for greenery or blooms around the border.

Bones Garden

Of all the garden architecture components, post-event garden bones are the hardest to integrate. Before you help fill out the information, you need to have a good base, like a house or a plot. If you've looked at a greenhouse where all the plants were the same height or scale, you've looked at a garden without bones. Small trees and shrubs are often used to shape the base of a landscape, and they are classic evergreens. You may not be able to get a hedge of evergreens as a background for your tiny frontier, but dwarf evergreens will do pretty good to create centering and a sense of permanence. They always do wonders to add fun to your backyard in winter, and draw birds.

Color

Color is the primary stumbling block for beginner garden designers. If they appear perfect in blueish-reds or orange-reds is interesting, so many people can tell you, but most of us couldn't realize the diff between the red roses. If you have affection in your garden for certain shades or an abhorrence of orange or red, you might already be on the path to an excellent selection of colors.

Focal Edge

Sometimes, when you're continuing to work in your yard, your mind's focus on the little things like the slug devastation on the weeds that sprang up recently. There are still citizens who won't be standing back for seeing their gardens like a fresh visitor might. Ideally, at one glance, you wouldn't want to fit in a greenhouse. That's going to be a light-hearted journey. Just having visual elements within your landscape is a simple way to do that. Large plants, houses, or decorations may be the key elements, and they aim to capture the attention of the eye and then direct it to the plants around it. Don't think your landscape is too small for a focal point. Containers should also hold a focal point.

Gravel and Path Stones

Gravel can be used in driveways and passages or even to line your lawns. Pathways can be paved with all sorts of materials: river stones, pebbles, bricks, flagstones, concrete slabs, and many others. You can create a quaint little passageway with rustic charm and storybook flair by letting the grass or weeds go wild and once it reaches the desired height, then plow a path through it. It is simple to do and even simpler to maintain. Dirt paths are also a cheap and simple idea for passageways.

Archways and Entrances

The outside of the garden matters just as much as the outside, especially in cases where it is completely enclosed and unseen from beyond your property line. Even from this vantage point, however, points of beauty can still be created as hints to what one might discover within the walls. Gates and entrances can be as elaborate or simple as you prefer. They form the first visual impression upon entering your living space-lawns, gardens, and yards included. You can use doors or gates as entrances within the garden as well. When you have secret walled gardens, gates can be a good idea for added mystery. They can be made from wood, iron, steel, or any other metal alloy.

Stairs, Steps, and Levels

One way of adding dimension to one's outdoor living space is through adding levels, especially in sloping areas. A prime example is the famous rice terraces of Banaue in the Philippines. The natives utilize the land effectively by creating flat levels of land where they can plant their crops. Similarly, one can utilize sloping areas and keep one's gardens situated in higher or lower places.

Fountains and Waterworks

A sure way to add interest in one's garden and to mimic the scenes in nature is to have a working waterworks system. You can have fountains in any size, with statues spouting water into a pool. You could have mini-waterfalls or simulated streams which, aside from being visually attractive, give off that gentle, soothing sound of rushing water. You could make use of an underground spring or river by building a well. Aside from being a possible water source, it could be a thing of beauty as well.

Ponds and Bridges

One way of getting close to nature is to create habitats for living creatures. One of the most commonly made is a fishpond. It is a great way to house your aquatic animal friends while creating little spots of attractive landscaping. If the pond or pool is big enough, one may even put in a bridge for better viewing and feeding of the fishes, and to get you from one side to the other. Having ponds is the right way of nourishing aquatic flora and fauna as well. You can have water lilies or lotuses to spruce up the surface of the pond or pool beautifully.

Animal Feeders, Habitats, and Baths

Aside from creating habitats, another way of attracting animal life is by creating feeders and baths. The most common one would probably be bird baths and bird feeders, but other types could be made to attract a wider variety of wildlife. Instead of putting birdfeed, you could put in nuts and grains for squirrels. You could make a beehive feeder to attract potential plant pollinators. With the types of plants and trees that you have in the garden, you can attract or repel certain kinds of birds, bats, insects, and a variety of small rodents. This is not a bad thing, as they can help in fertilization, pollination, and spread of the plant species.

Arbors, Gazebos and Small Shelters

You can create rooms with a view with the use of vines, canopies, and pergolas as the "walls" and "roof" of your outdoor room. Hide from the harsh glare of the sun with little shelters that provide well-needed shade during the warm months of the year. With a stable structure to grow on, plants can be used to create seemingly living walls that offer enough coverage for privacy and seclusion. You can create little spaces with intimate seating, that is an ideal setting for romantic dinners and dates. Roses can be grown on an arbor to form a natural roof that is all at once functional, beautiful, and sweet-smelling.

Hiding Places, Hidden Treasure, and Mystery

Create an aura of mystery by putting in little hidden treasures that are surprisingly pleasant. You can place a small fountain behind a hedge for example or put a miniature playhouse behind some tress at the very edge of your property. Guests will be especially delighted when they discover this treasure. You can hide secret gardens behind walls and fences for a little intrigue and to attract the viewer's curiosity.

Tunnels, Vines, and Trellises

You can create a green tunnel by training flexible plants to grow and form overhead. This not only gives an enchanting feel to the place but also provides needed shading from the sun when the opportunity arrives. You can use trellises to train vines to grow over the walls of your house, creating a sort of living carpet or wallpaper. Flowering vines can add color if green is not a particular favorite. Vines can be made to grow to make canopies that function as outdoor roofing for shade and shelter.

A Quiet Place for Retreat

There are times when we all need a break from the stresses of the world. You can create an avenue of escape by placing quiet little nooks for peace and meditation right in your garden or yard. You can put in benches, chairs, pillows, mats, rugs, or even a hammock or day bed to add comfort. Bamboo fountains, meditating stones, and crystals could be incorporated into the design for an extra calming effect.

CHAPTER 5:

What landscaping materials will You need?

Paving Materials

There is also the consideration of following a particular theme if that is a factor in your design. For instance, if you are going for a Spanish or Mediterranean theme, you could consider using large red or natural colored tile for the flooring. Brick is a traditional material used in Colonial-style homes. Flagstone, which is set in random shapes, can go with many different themes, as long as they are not too formal.

Flagstone and brick combination

Both are set on a reinforced concrete base for strength.

Concrete can be given a variety of textures and color blends. One of these concrete finishes is a stone-like texture with earth-tone colors. This particular finish also goes well with boulders and flagstone, and we use it a lot when going for a casual or natural feel.

If you want to design in such a way that the cost factor is kept from getting out of hand, there are a few things you may want to consider when selecting your flooring materials.

If you plan on hiring someone else to install the flooring, most tile, brick and stone surfaces tend to cost more than something like concrete; since concrete finish work goes much faster than laying each stone, brick, etc. by hand; so the labor is almost certainly much cheaper. Concrete usually involves just a single finishing step.

Also, paving elements like brick and stone often get installed over concrete to add strength, so you have the cost of the concrete, plus the cost of the stone or brickwork on both the material and labor side of things.

Manufactured brick, made to look used, was employed for the stairs to bridge the upper and lower patio areas, which are both concrete.

On the other hand, if you plan to do all the labor yourself, and you like brick, stone, or tile, and you want a permanent installation over concrete, you can avoid the largest cost of these items, which is the time-consuming installation. Also, since each brick or slab of stone is laid down one piece at a time, you can proceed at whichever speed works for you. The concrete base just has to be strong and flat and have the right drainage slope, but it doesn't have to look good. If you aren't in a big hurry, this could be a perfect solution. A professional looking brick or stone patio floor usually adds more value per square foot.

There are applications where brick and stone pieces are laid on a sand base or even simply set in the soil, but over the long haul, this type of installation doesn't hold up well, unless it is done with very high attention to detail. It could work for features like a small patio in a garden setting, rather than the main patio area—someplace that won't get a lot of traffic.

Rustic garden seating area with pieces of flagstone set in soil used for the flooring. This is a low-traffic area.

If you decide to go with a concrete slab, the question of tree roots and heavy clay soil, that tends to move a lot when it gets wet, may come into play on this. With concrete that is installed over a properly-compacted sand base at least two or three inches deep (to help prevent stress when the soil underneath moves), and with a steel bar and even the new micro-fiber reinforcing techniques, you are essentially betting that the concrete will be stronger than any of these forces. And if it is done right, you will probably win that bet.

You may also want to consider root intrusion from nearby trees in the interest of protecting the integrity of your patio. In this regard, there is a professional trick, which is called a root-barrier that can be employed. This is a thick, poly-plastic panel that can be installed around the root ball when the tree is planted. The plastic barrier forces the roots to go down into the soil two feet or so before spreading out. This product is used a lot now by city workers when they plant trees next to sidewalks, and it can be used for trees near the house foundation as well. It even works to reduce roots from surfacing on the lawn over time.

Another factor in containing cracks on concrete slabs is joints, which are cut in the concrete while it is still wet. These are the lines, every 6 feet, or so that you have probably noticed in sidewalks. These will purposely weaken the concrete where the joints are cut so that if cracks do develop, they are in the joints and are not noticeable.

If you want a lot of curves in your paving, concrete is certainly the easiest material to work with, compared with pavers, stone, and brick; since with concrete, you won't need to custom cut a lot of individual pieces.

Concrete can be done in quite a several finishes, and adding color to it is not a very big expense. Color can be added into the concrete mix or added on top after it has been poured on the ground.

For a natural stone feel using a textured finish, we normally use both methods together to get a natural blend of tones.

Texture-stamped concrete trimmed with used brick

Other finishes for concrete include exposing just a little of the surface to give it a sandy feel or exposing more of the surface to show some of the gravel (this last one is hard to walk on barefooted). Rock salt can be used to purposely pit the surface (the salt is washed away after the concrete is dry). Flat concrete can be given a very light broom finish to help prevent slipping when it gets wet.

A clear coat sealer can be used to enhance the color after the concrete is dry, particularly on stone-like textured surfaces. This also keeps water from penetrating the concrete. There is one important note on floor-sealers used outdoors, which has to do with safety rather than appearance. Some of the sealers can create a surface that gets very slippery when it is gotten wet —just like ice. This is especially true with oil-based sealers. A gripper substance, in powder form, can be purchased and added to the sealer before it is applied to prevent this from happening.

Pre-cast concrete paving stones (commonly called pavers) are another possibility and are intended to be set on compacted sand rather than concrete. They are often advertised as a way to avoid cracks. If installed right, with an adequately thick sand base underneath and proper compaction, and if the edges are locked in properly with the edge pavers set in concrete, this can be a viable alternative. The overall cost of this type of installation is usually comparable to the cost of colored and texture-stamped concrete, possibly a little more if you choose an exotic blend of pavers. One advantage to using pavers is that certain types can be a fair imitation to that cobblestone look that you see in Europe, without the big investment to install actual cobblestones. It is also true that they don't develop cracks like large slabs of concrete can over time, and if one is broken, it can be easily replaced.

Gray pavers were used in conjunction with the existing brick to expand the usable patio space in this backyard.

From a maintenance standpoint, a comparison could be made between a poured concrete surface and the pre-cast concrete pavers that are set in sand. The pavers tend to have a rougher surface, so it can be tougher to sweep clean. Also, when washing them, sometimes a bit of the sand that is swept between them during installation (used to lock them tightly together) can be dislodged and end up on the patio. Other than these minor nuisances, if the installation job is done correctly, the pavers do hold up well. On the plus side for pavers, if you like the advantage of that stone-look without the bigger price tag, and you don't want any potential of cracks, then pavers are certainly worth considering. If you don't want to pour any concrete at all, then pavers are a better choice than putting large random stone pieces in dirt or sand, as these will almost certainly lift and move over time, creating a tripping hazard.

Wood decks may be another surface worth considering. If the house is raised above the ground much, this could be the easiest solution for the primary patio. If you want to take advantage of a great view from a sloped area, a wood deck could be the most practical thing to build, or possibly you just like the look of a deck and want to put one in your design. Redwood and cedar are natural materials and will require some maintenance over time, but generally can last a long time.

Redwood deck built to expand the patio space out over a steep hillside.

New composite materials now exist, some of which are a good imitation of wood but without the maintenance. There are also a few exotic kinds of wood that are very hard, like Ironwood, and these are impervious to just about anything. Perhaps the most critical factor in building a deck that will last is to use treated timbers for the structure lumber underneath the deck. Just using standard construction grade Fir for the under-structure can lead to deterioration in a short period.

This is where we get into various overlay products. Some of these are just used for coloring, while others can be used to add a new texture to the floor surface as well. New ones are coming on the market all the time, but two companies whose products we have used to handle this problem are Elite-Crete and Brickform. Both are professional products that are way beyond old patio paint that tends to peel off in a year or two. The cost of this kind of approach is much less than the demolition and replacement of an old, tired concrete surface.

Flagstone was added to this existing concrete driveway by cutting parts of the concrete out in a curved design. The remaining concrete was left in place and stained with a blend of earth-tone colors.

There is a large variety of materials available for paving surfaces. The cost can vary a lot, and a trip to a building supply yard might be worth your time to see what is available in your area and what the price ranges are. Generally, building material costs more if it has to be shipped a long way, or if it involves a lot of hand labor to mine, cut, etc. Hand-cut slate usually costs a lot more money than tile, which is manufactured. Brick shipped in from another state might cost double what a local brick would cost. Quite in addition to looking at costs, though, spending an hour or two strolling around a building supply yard could spark a fresh idea that may not have occurred to you before.

Equipment

Nozzles:

The heart of any fountain display is the spray nozzle used to distribute the water. The effect that is obtained is directly related to the design of the nozzle itself, and this component requires precision engineering.

Pumps

Pumps used for fountains and pools are similar to those discussed in irrigation. A fountain system will employ either a centrifugal pump or a submersible pump since the water is taken directly from the pool and re-circulated through the system.

For fountains that require high operating pressure and large volumes of water, a centrifugal pump is usually the best choice. The major difficulty with the centrifugal pump system is that the pump must be housed somewhere near the pool, and this may be objectionable as well as expensive. Submersible pumps are usually employed for small fountains that have moderate pressure and water volume requirements.

Water Level Control Devices

There are two kinds of water level control devices used for pools and fountains: electronic and float type.

An electronic device is a small sensor that operates an electric solenoid value to keep the pool full. The float type device is similar to the assembly in a water closet. Water pressure acting on the float keeps the valve closed, but if the water level drops, the pressure is no longer on the float, and the valve opens. The electronic device is usually used on pools that have volumes greater than 1000 cubic feet. For pools of less than 1000 cubic feet, the float valve is generally satisfactory.

Filters

Large pools and fountains usually require the use of a filter system to reduce the frequency of maintenance. These filters are the same as those used for swimming pools and use sand charcoal or diatomaceous earth as the filter material.

Lighting

Pool lighting equipment is available in both 120 volt and 12 volt systems. The 12-volt system has the obvious safety advantage of providing little shock hazard; however, they do not have the wattage flexibility of the 120-volt fixtures.

The maximum bulb wattage for a 12-volt system is about 300 watts, while a 120-volt system can provide wattages in excess of 1000 watts, and the bulbs are longer lived. The lamps used for underwater lighting are not the same as those used above ground.

They are designed to operate at higher temperatures taking advantage of the water for cooling- This is important because pool lights will bum out if they are operated above the water surface- Other Fountain Equipment

Water jets

Water jets are the result of forcing water through a restricted orifice (nozzle) to increase its velocity and generate a uniform stream.

As we have noted in brief two basic effects are used in a pool is to have a single aerating nozzle the design of ornamental fountains; water that will operate at the height of 20 ft from the pool.

Most pool equipment manufacturers and contractors recommend that the fittings be cast or machined from red brass to ensure longevity and prevent leaking.

Lawnmower

Anyone who owns a lawn cannot have the luxury of lacking this tool; it is the most essential. Lawnmowers are available in different kinds, with a cylinder or rotary blades, and some can collect grass clippings as they mow. Mowers can be pushed or propelled, or gas-driven and the environmentally friendly mowers run on batteries.

String Trimmer

A string trimmer is effective for cutting grass that the mower can't reach; they are superb for cutting the grass around the walls. String trimmers can also be useful in lawn areas with tight and long grasses. They use a nylon string that rotates at high speed to cut the grass.

Edging Shears

A flawlessly edged lawn is an appealing component in the garden, and edging shears make trimming simple. All you need is to push the soil away from the grass edge and, after that, use the shears to cut the edges like scissors.

Turfing iron

This is a tool used to help expel turf from the garden after the square of turf has been mowed; the turfing iron is utilized to cut underneath it, separating the grassroots. It has a sharp point for slicing and a calculated handle that helps in producing level bits of turf.

Half-moon cutter

Used for making sharp, fresh edges or slick cuts, the half-moon cutter is designed to cut proficiently through the turf with level sharpened steel that guarantees a straight line. At the point when cutting an edge, pull a line of string and tail it with the razor-sharp edge, chopping in a descending manner.

Broom

Useful for a mixed bag of employment, it is a basic lawn tool. Utilizing a firm broom is one of the best routines for brushing top-dressing into the openings made by air circulation. Floor brushes are likewise helpful for clearing hard surfaces, similar to paths and patios, after grass redesigns, and for keeping the lawn flawless.

Besom

Frequently referred to as a witch's floor brush, this is a valuable distinct option for a firm sweeper since the coarse brushwood is successful for clearing leaves off the surface of the garden in fall, uprooting grass clippings in the wake of cutting, and clearing top-dressing into the gaps after air circulation. Besoms are not difficult to make. All you need is to tie brushwood to a strong wooden stick, for example, hazel.

Leveling rake

It is also called landscape rakes; these rakes are available in shops, and they are either made of wood or stainless-steel heads. At the point when setting up the ground for laying turf or seed sowing, they are utilized for the general leveling of the soil.

Spring-tined rake

These wire-tined rakes are utilized to uproot the dead bits of grass at the base of the plants, known as thatch. They ought to be used to scratch energetically the surface and ought to be utilized twice, in two distinct bearings. Spring-tined rakes can likewise be employed to expel leaves from the garden.

CHAPTER 6:

Landscaping Gardening Ideas

Types of Landscape Designs

The finest landscape layouts are indeed the ones meticulously planned out with an eye for detail. It is crucial to assess what design will best suit your residence and way of living before designing a landscape.

Continuing to work for how much you have is among the most valuable aspects of landscape architecture. E.g., if you are looking for a formal English garden, but your yard requirements do not match it, it will never turn outright. However, you should try to incorporate drought-resistant crops and dry elements into your landscape architecture if you reside in an arid region.

There are a couple of factors you can consider when deciding a landscape or lawn style:

What sort of environments are there in your yard? Is the place mostly cloudy or very warm?

Which style of scenery better fits your style of life?

Would you need a low-maintenance garden, or do you enjoy taking care of your yard most of the time?

Which style of a landscape would best enhance your residence?

Which type of activities are you going to use your yard for?

Who is going to use the yard? Would you consider having kids or pets?

There are various significant styles of landscaping and gardening, which you can then prototype your own. Alternatively, you can be inventive, incorporating elements from multiple methods to generate your design look.

English-style Landscape

The English Garden Design makes use of several shrubs and perennials in a scheme complementing your home's underlying theme. Other elements of decoration could include an arbor or a birdbath.

Oriental Countryside

Using a range of plants, the Oriental Style utilizes soil, bricks, and greenness to create unique viewpoints. You might even suggest incorporating a typical Zen Japanese garden.

Woodland Countryside

The Woodland Design represents the natural way fauna develops in a wooded environment with a less manicured look than certain other landscape types when you do not want to waste a lot of money on upkeep, that will be a smart option.

Formal Countryside

Of order, well-pruned crops, the Formal Style exhibits symmetrical patterns, clear lines, and complex geometrical elements. These landscapes often feature topiary design. This aesthetic of landscaping requires much maintenance.

Informally Designed Landscape

Informal Design utilizes edging curved plant beds. Plants are organized according to unrelated designs. If you have boys running in the neighborhood, this will be a smart idea.

Gardens of Butterflies

Dozens of the butterfly or species of birds that are native to your region make particular gardens a welcoming addition. Many plant species have a supply of calories and are useful to draw such flying mates. Creating free and wind safe areas.

The Jardine of Xeriscape

The yard or greenhouse consumes as many as 50 percent of household energy.

This practice for habitats involves plenty of low-water trees and plants and developing strategies to minimize moisture absorption.

Garden of the Mediterranean

This type of garden is wide walls lined with abundant olive groves, conifers, or cypress plants. Sometimes, a water feature or flowing water pond is needed. Splayed rosemary or other surface coverings that spill out of the walls or into big bags.

Lilacs are working well along or around buildings, as structured hedges. Plants that bloom a green, gray, or purple spikey flower can provide to this garden theme. Bougainvillea mounted around walls with light color.

Garden Cottage

This type is called a garden of old age. Try including the lilac, hydrangea, plum, and mauve plants. The perennials that we have listed will fit well with this style.

Herbs are also wonderful in a Cottage garden - rosemary, sweet bay, cranberries, and figs fit this garden-style perfectly. A neatly trimmed lawn with floating flowers at the bottom. It is a landscape with substantial upkeep, plenty of soil, and constant pruning and fertilization.

Bio Farms

As even more individuals learn the negative impacts of many toxic substances, naturally growing plants are becoming more prevalent. This implies the use of natural forms of insect management and implantation, rather than artificial fertilizers or sprays.

Consider if you have a landscape scenery you are pleased with, you will be spending considerably more time in your lawn. In addition, if you have a yard that you can frequently use, it is like having space in your house.

Choosing the Ideal Landscape Design

If your yard wants only fresh seedlings or a full refreshment, it can be daunting to overhaul the garden. For the ideal garden, here are a few should-know landscapes architecture ideas.

If you have never before attempted an outdoor space design, all of the options you may make can surprise you. However, if you speak about it within your home as space, it makes things even simpler. The same concepts, which guide the setup of your room inside, should also direct your designs outdoors. You are capable of managing a room together – so your scenery should not be a problem! Here are a few concepts for starters of landscape architecture.

Evaluate the Desires and Needs of the Landscape

Develop a "requires and wants" chart. Do your children require room to play? Want to raise vegetables? Would the family like to be assembled in a patio? Also, do some messy yard sketches with thoughts where you would like to put things in; it is a wonderful ideological basis for beginner landscape architecture.

Begin Small

Home and garden TV shows are experts at showing full outdoor makeovers in only three days — but they have a 60-member crew, which is not a condition most inexperienced gardeners love.

Way to create a landscape is working on a plan slowly and enjoying the challenge. Focus on a small flowerbed, from your grand plan. When you have the time, go out there and collaborate on it for two hours, and worry that much about clogging everything up immediately.

Write About Where to Go

Research the movements of Sun and Air. You may decide to put a deck on the south side of the building, but it will get loads of afternoon heat, which means September's dinnertime will not be soothing —just dry. So, a fire pit can soon be engulfed by wind bellowing across a corner. These are all common errors for beginners of landscape design. Whatever the wind and sun do at varying periods of the day and month should be taken into account in your design.

Hold Back and Admire The Landscape.

Live time with it. Getting too fast decisions regarding your yard will contribute to long-term decisions that do not function. Within a week of spending a lot of time outside, you are going to start seeing regions where you can go and take a seat that you did not even think about at first.

Emphasis on Size and Motion

It is the hardest principle for beginners in landscape design, but magnitude and pacing give a lifted-together look to your yard. Variations of scale, form, and color may arise, with tall plants against a house or at the rear of a flowerbed, and pathways taking pedestrians across space. Panovich stresses the importance of striking the right balance among reiteration and unique themes. Persistence gives a sense of coherence, but you do not want it to be boring and repetitive, either. A seasonal new option is a better option than having all the various elements at all. Every effective garden plan has a central focus or set of focal points, so it is a simple concept for beginners to apply in landscape design. That could be a sculpture or a beautiful flower, a shrub, or a trilogy of trees. Let the design roll your eyes across the countryside.

Be Accessible to Modifications.

Unless you are dedicated to something, be truthful about whatever you want and like — and what might fall out of your favor.

Patience is required for beginner landscaping. If all that space is just too much to look at, as well as the kids and animals track in dirt, rely on alternative fixes — annuals, ground cover, fast-growing surface coverings — to cover the ground while you are having figured out whatever you want.

Landscaping Ideas

Considering enhancing your back yard this quarter but worried about what it can cost? Get no concerns. It has heaps of cheap landscaping design elements to your garden.

Check these budget-friendly ideas to make your backyard garden beautified without taking out a home loan.

Use of Multiple Alternates

Mulching is a time and energy saver because it reduces the amount of water and requires mowing in the garden, but mulching itself can be expensive. That's why having a cheap mulch option for the project at the backyard is one of the better options. Substitute for better premiums on mulching:

- Grass Cuttings: The very next moment you mow, the cuttings and gains are put on the flower bed and raked up.
- Leaves: crushed leaves provide your plants with a nice, inexpensive replacement mulch and also fertilizer
- Wood Cones: A replacement for mulch relatively low maintenance, durable, and quick to scatter.

- Compost: Bring it to better use throughout your landscape if you've just made your first compost tank. Only beware of not covering it too thickly, since so much will heat up and destroy your plants.
- Newspaper: Let your plants take care of the humorous Sunday papers you've made – spread between four to six pages on the sheet, spray softly and cover with topsoil before planting.
- Sand: Sand mulch is not suitable for all flowers, but the weeding and maintenance costs will be popular in the long term if used correctly.

Former Tires Reuse

Tires are voluminous and can be hard to get rid of because many waste delivery trucks do not allow them. Why not put them back on your yard for good use? Here are a couple of cheap ways to landscape your yard using tires:

For a robust, rustic ottoman patio, cover with a pillow or corded patio enclosures.

Lined and installed tires to produce ornamental planters.

Build a hanging planter by attempting to fill one half of it with soil and add it to a wall or fence.

Create a groundbreaking indoor pool with a rim in the backyard.

Give your child a nice place to have fun with a reused tire climber.

Plant Upside-Down

Heart gardening but have little time or money to do it? Hold a clear setting in view. Vertical planting utilizes vertical space specifically placed for plant growth. The vertical gardens are a perfect starting point when you're looking for a budget for tiny landscaping ventures at the backyard. Not only can they make the most of limited resources, but they can also be inexpensive, particularly if you're using recycled materials such as old plastic water bottles. Following are the DIY planting ideas:

For a rustic vertical garden front porch using a wooden staircase, terracotta pots, and some cord.

Clean old bottles of paint, fill them with soil and bring them together to create a vertical herb garden.

To create a lush vertical greenhouse, using a photo frame again.

For an easy vertical zone to carry, a durable, unused footwear organizer.

Use several pot hangers and wooden screws to transform your fence into a vertical garden.

Apply a Spray-On Paint

Often what's needed is to add some hue to make a landscape glow. This can be as easy as painting plantings to give the garden a more modern feel or adding a new coat of paint to the wood, sheet metal chairs. Reuse the leftover paint from previous ventures to save still more on this current backyard flower bed, rather than purchasing fresh colors. A small splash of color may also be added in the form of plants or flowers, put on a balcony, patio, in an entry, or folded into a planting field.

Ground Feeding Stuffs

You can quickly transform your backyard from plants that repel pests into a beautiful and usable space with a couple of terracotta planters and the right location.

Creating an Open-Air Chimney

There's no easier way to get the kids around a fire pit. Yet you don't have to pay for a builder to bring one up – you can build your backyard campfire station in just a few minutes, with one ride to the home improvement store. When you choose to get out of the rocks from some other job, this is a perfect place to make a fire pit with them.

Planting a Tree

One of the simplest-and least expensive-tasks of any landscaping project is tree planting. All you need is just a few digging devices, every mulch, and the tree. Cultivating plants with excellent preparation in your yard will theoretically save you money in the long run.

Using Convenient Light Beacons

Cheap outdoor light bulbs are a favorite for backyard landscaping at a discount. In a chilling summer, the light, the atmospheric glow will make every patio meet. White sparkle lighting costs about $6 per coral, or you can even pick up a set of white horizon lights for around $9 for a more glamorous look. While globe light clusters are slightly more costly, they are usually more robust than sparkle light, and quickly substitute the bulbs.

Buy (or Make) Low-Cost Seats

If you have completed your budget landscaping programs at the backyard, you'll want a spot to kick back and enjoy the products of your labor. And the home furnishings shop doesn't have to make your own affordable home patio furniture run-you.

CHAPTER 7:

Design your home garden

How to Landscape?

When it comes to determining whether to plan your outdoor garden, there are just a few simple rules to remember. The fundamental idea that matches the purpose of the form is at the root of those concepts. The form and style of the space determine how you want it to be used.

First, you'll study these easy-to-follow ideas before you start "how to landscape," and then you'll be on the road to a beautiful landscape being created.

What are you doing, and what do you want? Are you waiting for a playground, a quiet place to read, or a mix of the two? You might want a spot in which to grow your favorite cooking herbs and vegetables. Make a list of your expectations and create a rough picture of how this situation is to be overcome. Following are the ideas that you have to keep in your mind to landscape:

Benchmark the Yard

Firstly, assess your yard. Which is The Way of the Sun? Build seating areas with shrubs and trees that are out of step with prevailing winds, or block and wind lead. Locate the sunniest areas and identify the right places to plant. Ideal for finding a place to rest and enjoy, shielded from the daytime heat.

It is also wonderful to build a room on cooler days and to take advantage of the sun's warmth. So, consider how you'd take water from one part of your yard to another. Start with sun angle measurements and establish a watering technique to know how and when to plant.

Exist in It

Staying in a bed is nice until we move in. Unless you sit in one place and spend time in one room or another, you don't realize whether or how that works in with your strategy. Turn back a chair to pick a new place to get up for the day. Notice potential focal points, and how they relate to your views of home and glass. How do known routes already function inside the mix? Paths that interact with the world impact the users' interactions, not just to direct them from one location to another, but to involve them as well.

Keep It Simple

Generally, the simplest answer is the best. No need to make the final decision more complicated or more extensive. Then, they have just the items that concern most. Start tiny and continue with a structure allowing you to easily switch to a flower bed, veggie plot, or patio from the inside of your home. Intuitive is still the right solution to the issue. If you overlook an actual walkway, for example, the direction, you built up through the lawn maybe a guide to the most convincing layout.

Loaned Opinions & key Points

Outside your yard, do not hesitate to take a drink in the view. Strategic positioning of trees to encircle existing views. Incorporating a tree as a focal point or a collection of trees to build new views. Sheltered plant trees offer bright colors in the autumn, in the summer. Find the flowering trees like dogwoods, buckeyes, crabapples, etc. Crop gardens, as well as perimeter forests, establish colorful focal points. To complement and enliven your outdoor experience, grow a collection of hydrangea-like flowering shrubs along with a patio or porch.

How Do You Want Your Plants?

A garden without plants is not a garden. Hold the plants you wish to expand on the running list. Then circle back to your site assessment to see what's possible. That will keep you in some shade from plants enjoying the sunlight. Assure that a watering plan is drawn up based on plant needs. Determine that equipment suits the construct well as having a heavy-duty hose with a watering thumb control nozzle and a timer.

Embrace Alteration

There's one thing that is discovered during years of rising and planting; it's that nothing remains the same. You can select a new route, or your patio is too narrow. And so your countryside is evolving and changing.

After pursuing these ideas and finding them, let's begin how to landscape.

Landscaping can make your block's front or backyard stand out from the others, and add value to your home. Figure out what kind of landscape design you're searching for, and then create a paper map. Then you should begin placing the plants into the field and install permanent attachments. Within no time, your outdoor space will be one that you want to spend time in.

Conceiving the Landscape

Set your budget for the scenery. Landscaping can be a costly undertaking, especially when the entire yard is complete. List things you want to install in your yard, or repair objects you like, and see how much it costs. Save $5,000-$10,000 USD, or 10 percent of your home's value, or get it into your landscape. If you do not want to invest a lot of money at once, focus a little bit at a time on the landscaping.

Matching Plants

Plants first. Plants grow environmentally friendly components, so you can build them accordingly. Find a spot on your yard to match your tree until it hits peak height. To facilitate transport and planting, find a young tree from the nearest nursery. Shoot an opening that is slightly bigger and wider than the tree's root network, then drop the flora to another surface.

Add the tree's root to bets to hold it straight stable and to discourage it from withering down. If you want shadows all year round in one's garden, choose green trees. If you only need the warm weather shade, choose the native plants which lose their leaves every year.

Built-In Fittings

If you want a good location, Then, exist in a garden. The patio seating may be built using a variety of objects and dimensions. Discuss how you plan to use the garden as part of your planning process and how many people you are planning to bring in. Use bricks, pavers, or concrete to shape your patio once you have an idea of what you should be doing. Have an open air-safe bench in your backyard, if you want a sitting area outdoors. Imagine a shade structure to be a morning relaxing spot.

Shaped garden walls to create beds. Build walls wherever you want. Drew a double trench, as deep as the doors. Fill the trench in with sand and rocks to build a strong, level floor. Locating the first stone document mostly on the ground, ensuring every single stone even exists. Fill in the back with gravel, stones, or some other well-draining stuff before you put up the partitions. Grow shrubs and flowers cut off in the area from your home, to start making your plants look bigger.

Landscape software

A lot of people claim tech is going to help them plan their landscape. With a degree, it can. Yet you 're always the developer, NOT the machine, and it can deliver exactly as you're asking it to. However, once you know how the app functions, you'll have the extra difficulty of studying how to use it and how to build it.

They believe that architecture software plans the landscape for you is like handing an instrument to a non-musician and asking them to play amazing music. I have absolutely no musical skill, nor do I have any comprehension of what creates music, music. I will certainly have received sound from every instrument you offered me, so what are the chances of making something tuneful?

Perhaps we'd be fortunate that it'd be a device with some pre-designed songs, so who'd want to listen to them? Even because certain computer software programs can come with a variety of designs already made, they may not be what you 'd want.

'Off the peg' prototypes you see in books and other tech products are impossible to match and become your garden of dreams. If you don't grasp the concept rules, you won't be able to quickly adjust them to suit the environment you have, in a way that fits.

Garden design software is great to show you how your garden looks like in 3D, and you didn't have to waste time drawing it. But it can often take ages to create a very basic type of design. Also, if a layout feature that you want is not in the software database in your garden, you'll have to find some way to get it in there.

I enjoy machines, gizmos, and tools, but I use a pencil and paper for design; obviously, it's a high-tech pencil, but still a pencil. For starters, I would strongly recommend that you do the same if you're already a whizz to CAD software. It'll save a lot of stress and energy.

Laying Out the Gardens

It is probably a good idea to touch on the subject of laying out the planting spaces, before going into details on specific plant choices you might want to make.

The first question you may want to ask is how much garden work you can realistically do?

If you have a busy lifestyle, yet intend to take care of the garden yourself, you may want to avoid too many big spaces, which need to be filled up with large quantities of plants.

On the other hand, planted gardens do tend to look best when they are layered, meaning the larger plant material toward the back, then the medium-sized plants in the center, and the small ornamentals in the front. It is not necessary to have the entire garden be this way, but rather, in places where you do have more space to plant.

Frequently, this is achieved by creating some planting spaces that are larger than the rest, particularly in the corners of the yard, and in areas where you would like to provide extra screening or special visual features.

Rustic flagstone wall supporting a raised garden. The treated wood stairs lead to the top of a waterfall.

Patios and walkways create natural garden borders. For planting areas next to a lawn, you can use an edging material to define the space.

You may want to consider the need for shade trees near any seating areas or to shade parts of the house. It is possible to put trees in the middle of lawn areas, but usually, they look best in garden settings, so you will want to allow enough space if you want trees.

Part of the garden space-layout can involve; anything in the distance you might want to screen, (where you can provide more planting area), and any great views in the distance you would like to preserve, (giving you a clue as to where the garden areas can be smaller).

You probably still want to use some layering of plants, even in the smaller garden beds, where feasible, so these beds should probably be at least large enough to contain more than one row of plants. You simply do the layering on a smaller scale.

In most cases, about 3 feet (one meter) is as narrow as you should go, and no more than 8 feet (2 ½ meters) is recommended for the bigger planting beds. This is just a general guideline that we have found to work in most cases. There are, of course, exceptions to this on both ends, depending on the effect you want to create and the space available.

If you imagine certain features; say a fountain or birdbath, a small seating area in the middle of a garden setting, or anything else you want to include in the layout, it is a good idea to add these into your design when drawing the lines for your garden areas, so you can ensure you have adequate space for them.

The extra room was created to highlight the fountain feature in this otherwise narrow planting space.

Curved garden lines naturally lend themselves to creating space for features. Weaving the lines out here and there will automatically create some larger spaces, allowing for layering your plant material in these areas.

Doing the same thing with straight lines tends to look less natural, particularly if you are framing the area with lawn. A large planting area done with straight lines, which suddenly juts out into the lawn, would tend to look boxy.

Large feature garden with smaller planting areas further along the wall. Curved lines naturally create larger spaces for plants.

There is one notable exception to this that can be quite striking; a design in which the patios and walk areas are all done in different-sized squares. When the gardens are all next to the paved surfaces and not a lawn, it can be a very interesting look.

This one can be a little more difficult to get right, but if you prefer the look of straight lines over curves, it can be an interesting design treatment.

The main point is to consider the overall needs of your garden design and adjust the shapes of the gardens before you get into the many small details involved in the plant choices. Completing the space layout first frees up your attention to focus just on plant selections and finding those special garden features to give the landscape your personal touch.

Patio and walkways all done in squares of varying sizes.

Practical Considerations

Let us admit it; it is a struggle to include edible plants in landscape design and to make it come out good. Sprinkling cabbage leaves, wild tomatoes, and scruffy peppers with bare seeds are the explanation that so many vegetable crops are confined at the farthest corner of the field – generally tucked away in only a few backyard beds.

With some simple shortcuts and suggestions, we are about to teach you how to do that in your yard. We discover that graphic examples of design features are the quickest way to get ideas, so we have collected a range of potential vegetable patch features/resources that you can use. Whether you are thrifty, inventive, just searching for ease fast, you will find solutions to match your time and budget like DIY, free / upcycled, and company choices.

Guidelines & Preparation - Creation of a Simple Edible Landscape

To plan your landscape, you do not need to be an artist or an expert at writing a landscaping blueprint. Many people create thorough to-scale drawings, and some only compose loose notes on a sheet of paper behind a scrap and then eyeball both until they get into the yard. Another smart approach to create an edible landscape design: consider a traditional landscape design and replace the plants in the design with edible plants.

Any drawing stationary + sheet of paper (or the unprinted side of last night's burger box) would do for this exercise when you are about to continue sketching! However, when confronted with the potential for new office equipment at the start of a worded project, unless you are some kind of individual who has to limit himself or herself from rolling about like a cat in catnip, here are some beneficial garden design techniques that go beyond guilty pleasures:

A journal for the "decomposition" of thoughts and drawings-a variation on a journal for the "composition."

A modeling stencil device suitable for edible landscape creation

Recycled Paint Sticks

Realistic Considerations for an Edible Design of the Landscape:

There is a realistic dimension of edible landscape architecture, besides the creative aspect of stuff. Below you may need to remember five important elements while preparing your edible landscape:

Microclimates

Know your yard's spots that get the greatest, and the least, sunshine. Using a compass or enter your address into suncalc.net (shade-casting items as if trees and buildings would need to be accounted for).

In summer, most vegetables and fruits take around 6 hours of sunshine per day to produce well. There are heaps of edible plants, however, which also grow flawlessly well in the shade.

Water Fountains

Where is your backyard water supply?

In drought spells, there may be an irrigation device, spigot, hose, dam, rainwater floodplain, or another source of moisture. You can haul a bucket to the far reaches of the yard, of course, but it is easier to prepare ahead, so it does not have to happen — and that you are edible garden remains well maintained.

Soil Issues

Where in your backyard are the most issue soles? Too hot, dusty, rough, muddy, flat, or filthy? Every position should be remembered. Try to solve these difficulties or place the garden somewhere else.

Note: Read more about Soil and Nutrients later in this chapter.

Ease of Access without Moving

Do not get through it! Part of having good soil and terrific garden design does never have to step into a bed for sorting, watering, harvesting, sowing, or whatever else. It induces compaction of the soil and is harmful to the plants.

Set of Plants

What plant types do you wish to grow? Most edible plants seek either a "meadow" setting (including most seed-grown annual vegetables) or a "hill" (often-woody shrubs and perennials on the understory). Remember because, after a tree falls, most forest plants are chancers who grow their best, and the ensuing canopy void allows them maximum sun for another few years. For safer crops and massive growth, you should build your beds to match those preferences. For starters, use heavy wood chip mulches; you might place your "meadow" beds in direct sunlight with lightweight manures of straw and leaves, and your "forest" grounds in maximum to partial sunlight.

CHAPTER 8:

Gardening tips and tricks for beginners

Where Be Will Your Garden?

The first thing you'll want to do is decide where the garden will be. Will it be in the ground or containers so you can take your garden with you when and if you move? (If you want it in containers, you'll then want to read how to care for your plants after they have been through a move to a new location.) Now, the second thing you'll want to do is figure out what you want to plant. Because the type of tree or flower you want will depend on where you plant it due to the amount of sunshine you get in a certain spot. The third thing you'll want to do is see just exactly what type of soil you have because again, the type of soil you have can be the difference between a successful growing season and a not so great growing season.

Feeding and Top-Dressing Methods

Fertilizer

There are three fundamental fixings to search for when selecting mineral nutrients for your garden: potassium (K) phosphorus (P) and nitrogen (N), which are generally expressed as a proportion of N:P:K. Nitrogen advances quick green development, as is regularly found in high amounts in spring feeds. Phosphorus is utilized to advance root development as is regularly present in high sums in fall feeds and pre-seeder manure. Potassium toughens up the grass, making it impervious to sickness, dry season, and low temperatures, as is regularly high in fall feeds. One other key fixing to pay special mind to is iron (Fe), which keeps the grass looking green without advancing abundance development. Mixes of manures and weed executioners can likewise be utilized, for example, garden sand (containing sulfate of smelling salts, iron sulfate, and fine sand), which kills weeds and later the weeds act as food for the grass when they decompose. The lawn can be fed by hand or use of a drop spreader or cyclone spreader in the large lawns.

Natural and liquid feeds

It is not only humanmade fertilizers that can be used on your lawn; there are normal, natural materials that can be utilized to encourage your garden. A mulch cutter slashes up grass clippings and disseminates them back onto the yard, in this manner returning nitrogen to the dirt. The bone meal makes a helpful phosphorus food, and fluid kelp is high in iron. Sprayed feeds enter the plant through the leaves, leading to quick results than dry manures, which break up in the soil and are then consumed by the roots. Manmade manure saves you from using your credit card, and it is also environmentally friendly to Make sure to encourage the youthful growth plants by feeding them using a can with a fine rose.

Top-dressing

Applying top-dressing to your garden enhances the nature of the soil, levels out surface knocks and hollows, and fills the gaps made by air circulation. Instant blends of top dressing are available, yet you can make your own by making use of sand, soil, and organic matter at a proportion of 3:3:1. Top-dressing ought to be spread equitably over the garden and after that brushed into air circulation gaps by use of a floor brush. For a perfect lawn, you ought to top-dress your grass every year in the fall

Watering

Sprinkling water on your lawn should not be done daily; it should be done on intervals. Watering your lawn routinely energizes weeds. Weeds have shallow roots compared to the grassroots; thus, by not watering so regularly, the grassroots go down deeper and deeper in search of dampness, and the weeds dry out since they are unable to keep up with the dry lawn surface.

Drought period

Amid times of dry spell grass stops growing, the cutting edges turn yellow and later brown before dying out, leaving the lawn bare, and the soil can vividly be seen. However, lawns can survive normal dry spells and will only need water if the drought condition is extreme and runs for an extended period. However, lawns can recuperate rapidly after the dry season and regularly make a full and quick recovery when it rains again. On the off chance that gardens must be watered, it ought to be done in the morning or night to lessen the loss of water through evaporation.

Consider the type of soil

If you need extremely rich green grass, knowing your soil type will help you decide how frequently you should water your lawn. Grass planted on loamy soils should be watered once every week and those planted on sandy soils twice every week. This is because sandy soil loses water quickly while loamy, and clay soil holds water for a longer period. When watering, water needs to penetrate down to the grass root system at least 4 inches down or 10cm down. To ensure this is done in the right way,, a small hole should be dug in the lawn to help check the moistness of the soil. You should avoid spraying water on the dry parts, paths, and patios to stop water wastage.

Watering Methods

Sprinklers

Keeping in mind the end goal to spare time, huge lawns are best watered with sprinklers, which can be clock-controlled to prevent water waste. There are many types of sprinklers available, including wavering sprinklers, which splash water from side to side and rotating arm sprinklers that will shower the lawn with a full 360 degrees. On the off chance that you have a little yard, you may need to utilize a handheld lawn nursery hose with a spray connection at the end.

Watering can

If your lawn covers small space, you may decide to use a watering can to do the watering. Although filling a watering can and carrying it will require more physical effort than using the hose to water. Watering can method helps prevent water loss than when using a hose or a sprinkler. If you have as of late sown grass seed, using a rose at the end of the watering can's gush will prevent the seeds from being washed away.

Mulching

Mulching is nothing but layering your topsoil with a mixture that will not only help you in controlling the weeds but also helps the soil in retaining the moisture content. This mixture can be either organic or inorganic.

Organic materials usually include leaves, tree bark, and felled plants, while inorganic materials comprise of plastic, **etc.** Ensure that your layer of mulch is not too thick. Remember to leave some room for the adjacent plants while you layer the topsoil with the mulch.

Mowing

Mowing a lawn is a requirement as it portrays its breathtaking beauty, however, cutting it short interferes with its growth. This leads to the grass utilizing all its stored nutrients to develop its sharp blade edges long enough with the goal that it can get more sun.

This weakens the root system, which makes the grass weak and efficiently stifled by weeds. Moreover, taller grass makes shade, and weeds do not develop well in the shade, so it is a natural obstruction to the growth of weeds in your lawn. Your sound grass will multiply and make a thick grass cover that will gag out weed

Weeding

If there are existing garden beds, then you must remove the weeds from these beds before you plant any new plants. If you are a beginner and not sure of how to get rid of weeds, here are a few methods as to how you can go about it.

This is the simplest way to remove weeds from your garden beds. It is all about identifying the weeds and cutting them out. Ensure that you uproot them completely as merely cutting their shoots will not solve the problem.

Sun

When starting any landscaping, first look at the landscape from the ground up. Soil is the most important aspect of any garden. Other aspects, such as if the garden is windy or protected, in the sun or shade comes second.

Know Your Soil

There are six types of soil: Clay, Silt, Sandy, Chalky, Peat, and Loam. As with each type of soil, there are different types of issues these soils have and what can be done to resolve the problems for better plant growth.

The first type we'll look at is clay, which tends to look like potter's clay when wet. When it is dry and rock-like cracking along the surface. One of the negative effects of this type of soil and is alkaline, which causes the roots of plants the inability to spread out and grow. (1) The second is silt, and its consistency is between chalky and sandy soil. The texture almost feels silky to the touch.

The third is sandy soil and has a light brown shading. True to its word, it won't hold water because it is made up of sand, at least for the most part.

Fourth, we have chalky soil, which resembles drywall dust. It has a white hue.

The fifth is peat, and it resembles dark coffee grounds and is fibrous and spongy. It also tends to be acidic.

Finally, six is loam, which is the combination of all soils.

Now we'll look at the problems and possible solutions for that soil. The first type of soil we look at is clay soil. (1) Because clay soil is dry, a way to improve it is to use sedge peat. Doing this increases moisture absorption, as well as relaxes the soil.

Once that's done, you can condition the soil so that it can be the best soil it can be. You can do these two ways: either use calcified seaweed or sulfur chips.

If, however, you don't want to (or can't) condition the soil with the methods above, you can still plant your garden. You'll just need to find flowers or plants that will grow in this type of soil. One plant that thrives in clay soil is the butterfly bush.

However, if you want to get dirt under your fingernails and dig into this gardening thing, you can improve this soil by combining enough peat and organic matter to the soil. You may need to cut it into the soil; you'll need three of each.

Now, if relocating your garden isn't an option, you may want to consider making a raised bed. For this, you'll need a ratio of 5 to 1.5 inches of topsoil to 1inch of aged organic matter.

The second type of soil we look at is silt. This is rich with nutrients but becomes waterlogged easily. Add organic matter such as compost or extremely decayed wood shavings or sawdust. To improve this, add 6 inches of this into the soil.

The third is sandy soil, which is found by seaside areas. This soil is high in salt and harmful to plant roots. Due to salt levels of organic matter, you might consider vegetarian matter such as aged grass clippings leaf mold, mushroom compost, or, and this is new to me humus.

Because hummus is cloud-like or fluffy in texture, it holds soil together, which creates a better environment, so the nutrients and moisture remain. For reference, moss that adds moisture is vermiculite/ sphagnum peat moss. It adds moisture, but not nutrients.

The fourth is chalky, and that looks just like it sounds like drywall. Peat moss offers both acidity and moisture absorption. When you begin choosing the organic matter, it'd be best to avoid mushrooms due to its more alkalinity, and it won't improve the soil's pH levels. (1). Instead, what you want to use is a bulky aged organic matter. This will pay off tremendously in the long run.

Now, to continue to treat this soil, you need to add sulfur chips because this of acidity it adds to alkaline soil. Ingredient amounts are three inches of both peat and organic matter worked into the soil.

The fifth is the easiest because you can use lime to neutralize the soil's pH level, making it more acceptable to various plants. After all, it is rare it's not dealt with in length. But many acid-loving plants can be grown in this type of soil.

And last is loam soil because it is a combination of the above five with a balanced amount of the first three. This type of soil is perfect for a great number of garden plants because it is high in nutrients as well-draining, and it offers a more balanced pH balance.

To give you an idea of these types of soil clay is like brown sugar, silt looks like powdered sugar and sand-like white granulated sugar. Loam is a combo of all of these types of sugars mixed.

Now a word of caution-Any soil can become depleted of nutrients over time, so using a quality of mixture of organic matter will benefit the soil in limited qualities.

CHAPTER 9:

Hacks for an amazing landscape garden design

Straight Lines and Curves

Creating lines in your garden can change the feel of the whole place. Straight lines give off an aura of order and symmetry. For minimalist styles or when going for a Zen-like feel, clean straight lines can help you achieve this goal. Curves, on the other hand, tend to be more free-flowing and uncontrolled. They work best when adding a graceful touch to your landscaping venture. Mixing up both straight and curved lines breaks up the monotony and gives an eclectic quality to the view. Line the sides of your driveway with flowerbeds and

follow its natural contour, whether curving slightly or going directly in a straight line. Create a pathway that starts from the outside of the garden and goes inward in a spiral that ends at the exact center. Contrast your straight plank fences with a wrought iron gate with swirling patterns and curls. Using lines and curves is not complicated. It is planting all your flowers in a row, or maybe arranging your lawn chairs in a semi-circle. It is that simple.

Shapes and Patterns

Be creative with the use of shapes in your garden or lawn. Do not limit yourself to the usual rectangular patch of green. Create bold statements with circles, squares, or even triangles. You can trim bushes into balls and arrange flowerpots to form ovals. Have fun with the grass on your lawn by creating patterns with squares to form an extra-large chessboard. Put in steppingstones that are arranged in the form of a wheel, or choose lawn ornaments that are all-round to follow a specific theme. Trim hedges into interesting shapes; take a leaf out of the Queen of Heart's book and create green hearts from your shrubbery. Use square blocks to form a wall or use ball-shaped planters to hold your geraniums. At last, there is a practical use for those long-ago lessons in geometry. Use it to your advantage and create shapes that were possibly never even seen before.

Contrast and Colors

Make use of your color wheel and get some bold and flashy results. Pair your greens with deep reds. Make the golden yellows of your favorite flowers pop out by putting them side by side with blue or indigo tones. The possibilities are practically endless! Make the left side of your flower bed with purely white-colored flowers and make the right side from red ones. Paint the front side of your fence with yellow, and the backside with black or brown for a subtle color changing scheme. Consider overflowing your flower boxes and plant them in shades that compliment your house color or that are in the shades of the trim color. Apple trees are examples of plants that show a beautiful array of leaf colors throughout different seasons, and an extra benefit has sweet apples to munch on during the fall or autumn months.

Avoid the blandness of placing plants form the same color group together. Create contrast by mixing in an opposing color from the color wheel to make them appear more vivid and striking. Using flora in warm colors creates a lively and happy environment while using cool colors keeps the feeling calm and peaceful. Colors can affect mood, and by using them for landscape design, you can create the perfect ambient feeling for every occasion.

Repetition and Symmetry

To create an effect of volume, place similar-looking or colored plants together in a clump. This would make for a unified and tied up look throughout the garden. Frame entrances with a pair of shrubs or line the hedges with one kind of plant. Use the same square patterns in your front garden that mimic the square patterns of your back garden. Put a flattering ambient light every five paces for gentle illumination in the early evening down to the deepening night. Flank the entrance to your driveway with twin statues that are like guardians who were sent there to protect. The point is to repeat one thing or one concept that would be the distinguishing feature of the whole landscape or part of it.

Keep the Cost Down.

Anything ongoing that you purchase is not going to be merely upfront costs. If you're going to buy something that will need special treatment to keep it the best that it can be, then you will need to be prepared to spend the money it is going to cost to keep it looking great.

There are a lot of things that you can learn to do yourself that will help a lot. Scoop out the pool and change the filter when it needs it. Measure the level of cleaner that you are putting in and keep it clean. Maintenance workers get paid a lot of money to do what they do, so if you want to cut down on that bill a little bit, it is important that you learn how to do it yourself.

Make it a Family Affair.

There is no reason why anyone person should get stuck with all of the maintenance of the lawn. Get your family involved in a fun and uplifting way, and you will be surprised at how much you can bond with each other when you are doing something as simple as lawn work.

You can assign different jobs to different members of the household, and work on completing the jobs all at the same time. This way, everyone only has a little bit that they have to do, yet you are still able to work together to get it done. It is quality time together, and profitable time spent working around the house.

Kids are great in the garden. If you don't have children, then work side by side, and you will enjoy some quality time together as you are making your plants and vegetables grow.

Create Your Hanging Basket

When you've got an old glass jar at home, making yourself into an eye-catching, drooping shelf is fun. All you need to do is add a covering, some fertilizer, a couple of flowers, and you're finished.

Look Outside the Current System

The primary target is an old shelf set for a budget-friendly seedlings cabinet or your indoor greenhouse. Make sure your seat is weather-resistant and will last for summers and winters, why not try to make it a lovely makeup with a paint pot and garden furniture?

Enhance the Garden Look with a Reflector

Think to light it with a weather-resistant mirror placed to establish a focal light where cobwebs were rarely seen before while a gloomy, rainy house remains. This may also offer the impression of space in a tiny, closed backyard.

Buy Synthetic Grass

If you are looking for a lush green garden, but not everybody has the perseverance to keep it trimmed and watered, then the remedy is fake turf. Usually, you can't be afraid to tell your neighbors what someone with envy needs to be so green, thanks to some super-realistic prototypes. Just be sure to give it a try, with a rough bristled rag every so often.

Grow your Companion Plants to Grow Specific Materials

Some preliminary testing is required for the user key. Strategically, neighborhood plants are based on what thrives well with others and can make survival possible. For starters, as the fragrance deters blackfly, well-smelling herbs like thyme grow alongside roses well.

Put Garden Technology to Use

When you can't rely on ensuring that your plants are well-tended and well-cared, it may be time to look at a pot of self-watering plants. There are loads of devices planted out there to make your land plot simpler to navigate. You might as well use an electronic pot these days!

Clearing Up of Floors

Now is the best time to do a quick scrubbing and spruce the deck or fix grass up. A power washer can do the job in so little electricity-and the change is so gratifying.

Make Your Deck a Place to Lounge In

We are building a living room much needs additional by continuing to invest in an outdoor sofa. Up the comfort level with luscious cushions, dining chairs, and an outside blanket, and get the most out of the hot weather.

Cheer up Empty Bench

Seek to move a new location into a landscape bench and build a nice environment where you can chill and rest. Dress it up with hundreds of cushions and a chair cover, and say you'll spruce it up with fresh colors if left untouched for years.

We love the sidebar, like a cooler cocktail that doubles.

Establish a Drinking-Station

Serve iced coolers with a Kilner-style, simple-to-fill soda dispenser placed on a wooden shelf while you're having fun outside. It's still fun playing, packed with squash and water for encouragement as the kids play in the yard.

Brickwork Mix

Give an old garden wall a facelift by seeding shrubs through its gap. Add grit to the planting location, push through the plant species, and then settle at last. Very seldom grow the sedums and sempervivums.

Choose What Seat to Turn In

This baffling seat can be enjoyed outdoor indoors with space to sit in for just one or two people. It makes statements of casual atmosphere, regardless of the environment, especially if you attach fake furs and velvet cushions for extra luxury on-trend.

Flowers or Bulbs in Pots and Tin

Why waste a ton on planter boxes when you can create a beautiful series with reclaimed jam jars and food tins? Only look at those harsh areas for sandblasting so you can wash them out. Try applying a sheet of stone blocks to the jar base, and the pop holes at the bottom of the tins for drainage.

CHAPTER 10:

Ideas for Edible Landscaping

Things to Consider When Having an Edible Landscape

Now that you've planned the list and cost of your plants, set out the final design. Just make your hand drawing design or have a professional send you the illustration. Some suggestions about architecture are as follows:

For wider spaces:

Including borders with anti-pestible flowers or berries

Introduce sizes by planting small soft-looking vegetables such as asparagus, as opposed to larger shrubs or trees

Enhance the visual effect of the whole garden by putting plants of the same color or type in one concentration, such as all yellow-colored fruit vines or climbers and flowers in the center of a lush green landscape;

For Gardening Containers:

Set measurements by placing larger shrubs in the center of the container and spreading herbs at the edges (use large tubes or wide baskets to achieve this effect)

Depth formation by placing potted plants in a layered holder

Improve the visual effect by painting pots in various colors, by using baskets or pots in different sizes and types or by planting the same colored plants on one hand

Take advantage of the advantages edible landscaping can offer. This landscaping alternative can be truly successful, from getting your own farmer's market to creating esthetic enhancement for your entire house.

Understanding Your Gardening Soil

To good land, a good garden starts. To have a safe, beautiful garden, you must make sure that you select a spot with nutrient-rich soil during your garden and landscaping preparation. Note, beginning with the soil makes improving plant conditions much easier over the seasons. Let's take a look at how the soil can be studied for your present or future garden.

Companions For Vegetables, Fruits And Planting For Flower

Vegetables are among the easiest and most rewarding plants to grow in your garden. Companion planting in the vegetable garden will boost physical performance and maximize both space and yield.

It is worth making a special note of the fact that members of the legume family (beans, peas, etc.) are a real asset to the vegetable garden. Because they are deep-rooted, they provide soil aeration for other neighboring plants while drawing their supply of nutrients from lower down. They also can convert nitrogen in the air into a form that can be consumed by other plants.

Try planting your vegetables in groupings rather than ordered rows. This has been proved to be visually confusing for annoying insects and also increases your chances of some of the vegetables going unscathed – while one group may be repeatedly attacked, others may be left alone.

Consult the list below to find good companions for your choice of common vegetables:

Alfalfa is a very good soil breaker. It is extremely deep-rooted, perennial, and virtually pest-free. It survives with only natural rainfall and accumulates minerals that improve nearly all soil types.

Artichokes are a lovely addition to any vegetable garden. They do well when planted with cucumbers. Keep artichokes away from potatoes.

Asparagus does well with carrots and tomatoes. Avoid planting close to potatoes, onions, or garlic.

Beans and other legumes enrich the soil with nitrogen when they die back and are therefore beneficial to many other plants. Plants such as corn that draw heavily on the soil's reserves of nitrogen are best planted along with beans. Beans will also grow well with brassicas (cauliflower, broccoli, and cabbage), beets, strawberries, cucumbers, potatoes, or celery. Do not grow runner or pole beans with beets – these two will be detrimental to each other.

Beets are known to enrich the soil with minerals and make good company for lettuce, onions, cabbage, and broccoli. For an improved flavor of beets, grow along with garlic. Mint is also a good companion, though it may be invasive.

Carrots are a good company plant for many vegetables such as lettuce, radish, onions, and tomatoes. Leeks will repel carrot fly, so plant them close to carrots. It is important to note that tomatoes may stunt carrot growth. However, this will not impair flavor.

Celery is beneficial to members of the cabbage family because its scent repels the white cabbage moth. It is a companion crop to tomatoes, beans, onions and leeks. It also does well in flower gardens when planted along with snapdragons, daisies, and cosmos. Do not plant celery along with aster flowers or corn.

Corn draws a lot of nutrition from the soil. Plant corn along with beans, as the latter will replace the nitrogen in the soil at the end of the season. A spreading plant such as pumpkins or melons does well plant with corn and helps to retain the moisture in the soil. Other companions include potatoes, parsley, cucumber, squash, peas, or sunflowers. Pig's thistle is renowned for drawing nutrients up from the subsoil, so when planted with corn, it brings them up to where the corn can access them.

Fennel is one plant that acts negatively on most garden plants. It kills a lot of other species. Dill is one of the few that can survive in close proximity. It is, on a brighter note, an excellent flea repellant – hence the old saying of "fennel near the kennel." It also attracts many flying pollinators and ladybugs.

Horseradish is a good companion for potatoes, as it is known to increase resistance to disease.

Lettuce, an all-time favorite, does well in the semi-shade of sunflowers. It grows well with other vegetables such as carrots, cucumbers, and beans. Avoid planting near cabbage – cabbage will deter growth and impair flavor.

Onions are good companions for leek, lettuce, beets, tomatoes, and strawberries. Chamomile will improve the flavor of onion. Also, when planted along with strawberries, onions will help fight diseases.

Peas, a member of the legume family, are excellent for infusing the soil with nitrogen. They do well in the company of the most common vegetables. Do not plant close to onions, late potatoes, chives, or grapes.

Potatoes are good company for corn, beans, brassicas, onion, and carrots. Flowers such as marigolds will benefit potatoes, and alyssum will provide living mulch. Do not plant potatoes near tomatoes, as the two tend to contaminate each other with early and late blight.

Pumpkins are an old-fashioned favorite for baking, soups, and pies. After harvest, they can be successfully stored in a dark place for a long time. Pumpkins do well when planted with squash, melons or corn. Remember that pumpkins take up a lot of room, so allow sufficient space for spreading. Dill and oregano will provide general pest control.

Radishes may well be called the 'hard workers' of the garden. They attract many insects and bugs away from other vulnerable vegetables, without damage to the root of the radish. They deter rust flies, borers and cucumber beetles. Radishes act as a lure for leaf miners and flea beetles. You can plant radishes liberally among spinach, squash, melons, cucumbers, beans, and carrots.

Spinach needs a certain amount of shade and therefore benefits from that provided by potatoes and bush beans. Spinach is a good way to maximize space when planted along with spreading plants such as squash – by the time the squash needs the space, the spinach has finished producing. It also grows nicely with members of the brassica family, onions, strawberries, and peas.

Sweet potato is a good companion for root crops such as parsnips. The sweet potato weevil can be repelled by the planting of summer savory. Do not plant close to other spreading plants as they will compete for space and sunlight. It also grows well with many of the aromatic herbs, such as dill and oregano.

Companions for Fruits

Picking fruit from your garden is a very satisfying experience. Apples, stone fruits, berries, and melons are easily grown at home, loaded with goodness, and also make a lovely gift. By carefully choosing companion plants for your fruit bushes or trees, you will increase yield and deter insects.

Cucumber is excellent to plant with beans and corn. All three plants thrive in the same conditions – full sun, plenty of water, and rich soil. Corn will provide a climbing frame for the cucumber. They also do well near radishes, beets, carrots, and peas. Try to avoid planting too close to potatoes and sage.

Grapes are benefitted by many of the herbs such as basil, hyssop, and chives. Planting grape vines beneath Mulberry or Elm trees has also been proved to be beneficial.

Melons grow well in the company of corn, beans, and pumpkins. Oregano will benefit melons by providing general pest control, and marigolds will deter various types of beetles. Nasturtium will also deter uninvited bugs and beetles.

Peaches are very susceptible to the peach tree borer. Garlic will be a great asset for repelling the borers. When planted in close proximity to peaches, asparagus, grapes or onions will also do well.

Raspberries reap great benefits from the close planting of garlic. Garlic stores Sulphur and acts as a fungicide for raspberries. To help repel the menacing harlequin beetle, interplant with turnips.

Strawberries are good friends with beans, lettuce, thyme, and spinach. Thyme, which makes a pretty border plant, will repel harmful worms. Borage is known to increase disease and insect resistance.

Sweet Peppers are best planted in the company of tomatoes, carrots, parsley, onions, and petunias. Okra is a fantastic windshield for these more delicate plants. Bell peppers make a delightful ornamental, so try including them in your flower beds.

Tomatoes are an all-time favorite and a 'must-have' in the most home vegetable garden. They have many allied plants: onion, mint, cucumber, basil, beans, and marigold are just a few. Keep away from potatoes, apricots, brassicas, and fennel. Walnut wilt attacks tomatoes if they are planted beneath walnut trees.

The corn earworm may attack both corn and tomatoes, so keep them apart – that way, at least if one crop is affected, hopefully, the other won't be.

Companion Planting for Flowers

A flourishing flower garden is, without doubt, the desire of many an avid gardener. By thoughtfully implementing the principles of companion gardening, you can maximize the health and productivity of your flower garden. The results of careful planning will soon pay off, and your garden will be the envy of many.

Why not try the theory of 'decoy' plants? If you have a particularly pest-prone plant, try planting a similar-looking. Still, hardier one alongside it – the shape and color of these decoy plants can visually confuse the unwanted pests. Nasturtiums are one of the most popular decoy plants. They seem to have a magnetic attraction to insects, drawing them away from plants which they would otherwise harm. Plants such as these are sometimes known as martyr plants because they suffer at the expense of others.

Many of the beneficial flowers which are good to include in your garden are easily grown from seed. Most garden stores seeds for marigolds, cosmos, and echinacea, all of whose flowers are irresistible to many of the pollinators.

The varieties listed below have unique companion properties which are good to keep in mind:

Chrysanthemums are a perennial favorite, of which some varieties are known to repel beetles. Costmary, a variety of Chrysanthemum, is known to deter moths.

Dahlias are a beautiful feature commonly planted in flower gardens. Their large flowers are delightful and repel nematode worms. Being a taller and bushier plant, they may be used to provide wind shelter for more fragile varieties.

Geraniums are perfect for repelling beetles and cabbage worms. Plant them freely around roses, tomatoes, and corn. They also help in the distraction of beet leafhoppers.

Gladiolus is best kept away from cucumbers, melons, and clover.

Larkspurs are beautiful, tall, spring-flowering annuals that will provide a dazzling backdrop for low-growing hedges or borders. While they are a delightful addition to your garden, they are also a healthy one; they attract Japanese beetles, which die after consuming them.

Lavender is an old English favorite and is renowned for both its beauty and fragrance. Lavender can easily be hedged, used as a backdrop, or simply placed among other plants for contrast. It is known to deter fleas and moths and, when planted under fruit trees, will help repel codling moth. Because it is a prolific flowerer, it attracts bees and other pollinating insects, which will benefit neighboring plants.

Marigolds are perhaps one of the most commonly known pest deterrents; however, they must be one of the scented varieties to be of any assistance. They do keep the soil free of harmful nematodes, which makes them valuable assistants to many plant varieties. You can plant marigolds freely throughout your garden, keeping in mind that they do tend to attract slugs and spider mites.

CHAPTER 11:

What are good ways to maintain home garden and landscape?

Your abilities

Before you begin with the landscaping, understand where your strengths lie. Take stock of your abilities when it comes to gardening. If you have had any prior experience when it comes to gardening or construction, make a list of your strengths, as these will help you to decide what is doable. You might wonder why this is of any relevance. When you take stock of your abilities when it comes to gardening as well as landscaping, it makes it easier to decide if you need to enlist the help of a professional or not. It also determines the time and effort that you need to invest in the entire process. Apart from your gardening skills, you have to take into consideration your sense of color and texture. Since landscaping is all about the magic of colors and textures placed side by side, you must have a clear sense of how you want your garden to look before you start working on it.

Commitment

Landscaping your garden can be a time-consuming process. It might look simple and exciting in the beginning, but it requires a good amount of effort on your part, especially if you have decided to do it all by yourself. Do not commit to landscaping if you can't cope with the hard labor involved. Rest assured that your hard labor will be rewarded, but be aware also that it's going to require physical input. Understand what this task demands of you before you start, as you may need to help with the physical aspects and hard landscaping.

Planning

Nothing is as important as a sound plan when it comes to landscaping. Why is this so relevant? When it comes to landscaping, if you don't have a clear idea of how you want your garden to look, your efforts will be futile. When we refer to planning, it means two things – planning the way you want your garden to look and planning your time to achieve the work required to get it into shape.

Colors and textures

Pick out the color scheme carefully. Landscaping is not about growing plants in all possible colors. It's about making a garden look elegant, even if there aren't many colors. Bear in mind that not all plants will look the same in all seasons. Choose your plants in such a fashion that they adhere to a certain color scheme during a specific season, as it is not possible to make your garden look colorful during all seasons. It is worthwhile listing the flowers and noting down the seasons when you can expect flowers to appear.

Textures add an interesting twist to the way your garden looks. Arrange your plants in such a fashion that there is some continuity when it comes to the textural aspect. For instance, it would look spectacular if you plant your rose bushes in the same row. This will look esthetically beautiful and also help you in effectively tending.

Ambiance

Apart from the esthetic features of your garden, the ambiance also has to be taken into consideration. The question that you should ask yourself is, "What should I feel when I step into my garden?" For instance, if you wish to have a peaceful and soothing ambiance, you could make room for a small fountain in your garden or a place to sit and enjoy it.

Other things that you could add to your garden to influence the ambiancc of it may range from interesting sculptures to walkways, lightings, **etc.** If you are going to invest in lighting, ensure that you have a clear idea of what you want the lights to illuminate. For example, you may be thinking of pathways or even highlighting certain species of plants. Choose them wisely and make sure that if underground wiring is required, this is planned for in advance. Many people use solar power these days, which doesn't require underground wiring.

Understanding your plants

An important aspect of your garden is the kind of plants that you wish to grow. Landscaping is not about growing all kinds of plants together. It's all about choosing those plants that are compatible in terms of needs, as well as that complement each other esthetically. Why is it important that you understand your plants? Sooner or later, you will realize that tending to these plants requires a lot of time and effort. If you choose companion plants, half of your burden is reduced.

Understand what the requirements are when it comes to different kinds of plants. Some might need a lot of sunshine, while others might grow well even in the shade. Landscaping is all about placing your plants in a strategic way that, apart from making your garden look beautiful, makes it easier for you to maintain it.

Do as much research as you can. List of all the requirements associated with the various plants. Choose those plants that are possible for you to tend easily rather than giving yourself hard work. A lot of time has to be invested in tending to certain species. As mentioned earlier, the time factor has to be taken into consideration.

Be open to changes

You might have to change the way your garden looks from time to time. Understand that your landscaping is not a permanent process. You might have to change some elements of your garden to suit the various seasons or to give your garden a new look. Be prepared for the changes, and expect your garden to evolve.

Get your family on board

You must get your family on board with the whole idea of landscaping your garden. As mentioned earlier, landscaping is a time-consuming process and requires a lot of manual labor. Unless you get the support of your family, it will most certainly be a Herculean task.

Keeping the initial landscaping aside, you would need an extra pair of hands in maintaining the beauty of your garden. Some families even allot different chores within the garden to family members, and this is worth thinking about.

Treating Bald Spots in Your Lawn

Garden care fans know how a single uncovered spot can make a delectable lawn look exhausted and inadequately maintained. A bald spot can stand out like a sore thumb while a few bare spots can compromise the beauty of your home.

Treating bare spots commonly relies on the cause of the bald spot. Bugs, dryness, pet waste, killer weeds, and harm from mowing are a percentage of the most primary reasons for bare spots. The following gives a breakdown of these diverse causes and how best to address every circumstance so you can restore your garden to its natural magnificence.

Controlling bugs

Often with a good jet of water, a plant may be wiped away free. Many garden centers are marketing bugs such as ladybugs to rid themselves of bugs and worms. Toxins are an alternative, too, but, when using them, use strict care. Take into account using "natural" in-household substances for insect control. For starters, putting a submerged plate soaked in beer in your insect-infested landscape would typically draw certain pests and destroy them.

Weeding

The only effective solution is to get rid of it is to cut the whole plant by the roots. Fertilizers do operate but implement vigilance. That way, you are going to destroy not just the herb but other surrounding plants as well. Hold weeds to a minimal by making a foot or two of mulch cover the surface.

An inch-thick mulch layer will keep your planting beds comparatively free from weeds. The grass is a plant that, when healthy, grows dense and bushy and will generally suffocate out certain weeds. Any inorganic fertilizers start with a "pre-emergent" that destroys the seeds while the plants are inactive in the morning.

Making moves

Do not cut the grass too early while it is too short. Lengthier vegetation is safer, in addition to which it also absorbs sunlight. Most mowers come with a choice to mulch, which cuts grass into tiny pieces and adds them to the field. It contributes essential nutrients to the soil and lessens fertilizer requirements.

Removing leaves

Clear the leaves off grassy fields. The surface of leaves will limit the intensity of the light near the roots to the lawn and to collect water.

Hedge trim and tree trim

Seasonal pruning is expected of trees and shrubs. Prune off old trees as well as active branches that get out of hand. In the season, several hedges ought to be post-shaped many times but rarely prune or cut during the fall. It would promote development at a period when plants are supposed to be inactive.

Elements of compost

It is important for landscapers to know about the composting process, what raw material to use, and how to use the finished compost.

Air and Space: Regularly turn your compost pile to aerate and manage this material properly. The turning process helps the decomposition process and supplies oxygen to the compost. Turn your compost pile every few weeks.

Moisture: Adding an adequate amount of water to a compost pile increases microorganism growth. Only add water if the compost pile is dusty or very dry.

Heat: Heat is another important factor in the decomposition process. Heat kills harmful weed seeds and pests and accelerates the decay process. The combination of moisture, heat, and oxygen all increases the presence and growth of helpful bacteria and fungi.

Products to compost: In addition to oxygen, heat, water, and space, you also need products to compost. Use kitchen waste such as coffee grinds, vegetables, leafy materials with leaves, wood chips, and grass clippings. These products will produce compost that is appropriate for a wide variety of plants. For better quality compost, use grass clippings, clean leaves, and organic kitchen waste.

Pruning

Pruning animates development, concedes air and light into the inside of plants, evacuates broken or unhealthy parts, and aides the plant into rounding out its common shape. Normal pruning adds to plant wellbeing and garden-style as follows:

Control tallness and width of plants

Guide development example and common shape

Forestall excess (which can cause infection or breakage)

Increase flower creation

Improve limb structure for quality

A few cultivators do practically the entirety of their pruning by hand since hand pruning, additionally called "punch pruning," is more beneficial for the plant. You have likely observed planters dashing around a property using shears.

That method is quicker; however, it just trims off the new development on the outside of a plant. After some time, the inside of the plant may get congested and thickly pressed. Light and air can't infiltrate. Also, that can cause ailment.

You ought to envision what the plant will do. If you realize a shrub regularly grows 18" during the season, and you need to keep it at windowsill tallness when it's blossoming, then you cut it back 18″ beneath the ledge while it is as yet lethargic.

Sustainable lighting for low-cost landscaping

Use energy-efficient lighting to contribute to the sustainability movement and save money. Light bulbs such as light-emitting diodes (LEDs) and compact fluorescent lamps (CFLs) cost more, but they have a longer lifespan than standard lights and save money by reducing energy bills.

Solar-powered landscape lighting is becoming popular. They are easy to install and relatively inexpensive and come in a wide selection of styles and colors. These lighting products cost more upfront but pay long-term dividends through saving time and money and contribute to protecting the environment.

Water

It is very important to ensure that your garden landscape remains well watered. Most gardens require water regularly to enable growth and to remain healthy. When organizing your garden landscaping, ensure that a good underground watering system is installed. The water demands of different areas of the garden could require different water allocation. Therefore, this needs to be addressed when designing the underground system as you might need more than one series of pipes. For instance, some plants do well in dry areas and require less water to survive, while others require a lot of water to stay alive.

Fencing

The location of your garden will determine if you need fencing or not. For instance, if there are animals that may access the garden and eat or destroy your plants, then you need to have a good fence or a ha-ha put in place. You may also need a good fence to keep your pets out of your garden.

There are other instances when you may not require a fence, but a good boundary would work well. You may use rocks to create a boundary that will protect the garden landscape.

Pathways and entrance points

You will need to access your garden from time to time. This means that you need to have access points that will grant you free movements.

Without proper pathways, you may end up stepping on and destroying the plant life and disturbing the soil. To properly maintain your garden landscape, ensure that you use your pathways to access the gardens.

Pest Control

You may encounter issues concerning pests from time to time. If you don't watch out, these pests will attack your plant life and destroy the garden landscape that you have worked so hard to create.

You can remove the pests manually or using pesticides. However, you have to remain vigilant at all times to ensure that this problem does not get out of hand.

Soil Care

Cultivators frequently dismiss the effect soil has on the wellbeing and power of their plants. Soil planning isn't the most exciting part of planting a garden; however, it's one of the most significant. If your soil isn't right, your garden will battle to arrive at its maximum capacity.

A garden is an impression of the nature of its soil. Nurseries loaded up with lovely soil have an imperativeness about them that we can nearly feel.

Accomplishing that essentialness requires understanding the science and structure of your soil and making the ideal condition for ripe plant development. Great soil management is a ceaseless procedure; however, once you take care of the nuts and bolts, your soil will do the vast majority of the work itself.

Conclusion

Landscaping is a blast, and if you see it as a journey and a progression to work at until you reach the end, then you connect with it! Then when you finish, it is that much more of an amazing experience!

Landscape architecture requires a designer who is imaginative and inventive. Preparation and construction will take environmental and architectural considerations. A skilled architect works methodically on every level and creates wonder in the locality in the form of beautiful environments, public parks, pathways, and gardens. They are not only adding importance to the commercial side but also enhancing their lifestyle.

The interior designer has to take control of all those things. Yeah, the thing you have to do is only choose the right interior decorator in your region anytime you decide to do imaginative landscaping. Landscape architecture and landscape designs have their own concept, and each of them has its own style and characteristics. We need to admire all of the old frameworks that apply to a new design which will suit our age. Landscaping has its places, from people to the climate. There are two elements in landscaping, which are hardscaping and soft scaping. A comprehensive overview of landscape ecology is provided in this text. This guide could be used by those who want to plan their yard beautifully. This guide also describes how such principles are to be applied in actual life.

If you talk about landscaping, in brief. Be sure you learn about it very well; otherwise, hire a landscaping professional for a small budget, he'll do the best job for you.

Landscaping and gardening is a lot of fun; there is no doubt about that! But it's even more enjoyable when you can do it in a cost-efficient way.

The main thing that holds people back from getting into landscaping is the fact that it costs too much, but if you use the methods we talked about in this book, you won't have to worry much about the cost!

So, if you want to employ a skilled landscape designer, formulate a plot map of your land, including your backyard or front yard is among the first items he/she will do. I hope this book was able to help you to fulfill your dreams of creating your perfect yard or garden.

These ideas regarding landscape architecture are important to the design of a scheme that you will appreciate in the years ahead. You can get these ideas about garden designing and landscaping from the following procedures:

See what a lot of people do with their home design designs. If appropriate, speak to them about the reasons behind their choice for home landscaping products, and their feelings.

Newspapers, magazines, television, and the internet do provide a wealth of information regarding what "online" types of home landscape designs are.

Ask specialist consult for the area of landscape architecture

If you don't want to pay for guidance to a landscape planner, try some tips from your nearest nursery, at least.

Printed in Great Britain
by Amazon

49916001R00061